After a few years, it starts to look beautiful.

"Ugly, isn't it?"
"No class."
"Looks like an afterthought."
"Good for laughs."
"Stubby buggy."
"El Pig-O."

New York Magazine said: "And then there is the VW, which retains its value better than anything else. A 1956 VW is worth more today than any American sedan built the same year, with the possible exception of a Cadillac."

Around 27 miles to the gallon. Pints of oil instead of quarts. No radiator.
Rear engine traction.
Low insurance.
$1,799* is the price.
Beautiful, isn't it?

BOOKS BY MARSHALL McLUHAN

The Mechanical Bride:
Folklore of Industrial Man
Understanding Media:
The Extensions of Man
The Gutenberg Galaxy:
The Making of Typographic Man
Verbi-Voco-Visual Explorations
The Medium Is the Massage
(with Quentin Fiore)
War and Peace in the Global Village
(with Quentin Fiore and Jerome Agel)
Through the Vanishing Point:
Space in Poetry and Painting
(with Harley Parker)
Selected Poetry of Alfred Lord Tennyson
(Editor)
Voices of Literature:
Volumes One and Two
(Richard J. Schoeck, Co-editor)
Counterblast:
(with Harley Parker)
The Interior Landscape:
The Literary Criticism of
Marshall McLuhan 1943-1962
(selected, compiled, and edited
by Eugene McNamara)

Culture Is

Our

Business

Marshall

McLuhan

Culture Is

Our

Business

McGraw-Hill Book Company, New York·Toronto

Library of Congress Catalog Card Number: 78-95817
45437

Art Direction: Harris Lewine
Design: Alan Peckolick

AUTHOR'S NOTE

This book is not about ads, but about our time. However, if some archaeologist in some remote future were to get access to the ads that appear in this book, he would consider himself very fortunate.

Ads are the cave art of the twentieth century. While the Twenties talked about the caveman, and people thrilled to the art of the Altamira caves, they ignored (as we do now) the hidden environment of magical forms which we call "ads." Like cave paintings, ads are not intended to be looked at or seen, but rather to exert influence at a distance, as though by ESP. Like cave paintings, they are not means of private but of corporate expression. They are vortices of collective power, masks of energy invented by new tribal man.

The twentieth century, the age of electric information, instant retrieval and total involvement, is a new tribal time. If Gutenberg technology retrieved the ancient world and dumped it in the lap of the Renaissance, electric technology has retrieved the primal, archaic worlds, past and present, private and corporate, and dumped them on the Western doorstep for processing.

Today, through ads, a child takes in all the times and places of the world "with his mother's TV." He is gray at three. By twelve he is a confirmed Peter Pan, fully aware of the follies of adults and adult life in general. These could be called Spock's Spooks, who now peer at us from every quarter of our world. Snoopy has put man on the moon and brought him back. Four years old may already have become the upper limit of tolerable emotional maturity. (This is not a value judgment. E.g., it would have been self-defeating for me to have said years ago "the medium is the mess-age": such judgments distract attention from the events and processes that need to be understood.)

Business and culture have become interchangeable in the new information environment. Social navigation and survival depend on recognition of the processes, and knowledge of the diversity of environmental "rim-spins" and epicycles that we have created by our own innovations. When a fast cultural spin is put around a slow one (e.g., when instant radio software is put around cumbersome nineteenth century hardware), the slower hardware breaks down. When the teletype letter or the telephone by-passes the old postal service, the older service breaks down. Since Sputnik, the planet has become a global theatre under the proscenium arch of man-made satellites. Our psyches acquire thereby a totally new rim-spin.

In the world of the new global theatre, everybody has to "do his *thing*." Role-playing supplants job-holding just as knowledge supplants experience. Newton discovered not gravity, but levity (outward pull). The reader of this book will discover much levity in the patterns of force of ads that shape and mirror our time.

These richly significant forms are easily obscured and destroyed by the classifiers and moralizers who want to know whether they are a "good thing" or a "bad thing." There are many educated people who consider it a bad thing to study or to understand what goes on in our world. This book is not for motivated somnambulists.

Contents

1

Flip

The conflict between the new "inner trip" and the old outer trip in truck or jalopy is characteristic of the larger flip in our current society.

A HANDFUL OF PILLS

"Psychoanalysis is vanishing," says Dr. Szasz. "The bark is still there, but the molars are gone." (<u>N.Y. Times</u>, Aug. 4/68)

Tranquilizers enable people to persist in their ordinary activities while leading lives of howling desperation. Anaesthetics also permit operations of fiendish torment beyond the dreams of the ancient torture chambers. The pain comes later. It is called convalescence. Before anaesthetics the extended torment of convalescence was unknown. The patient died at once.

Message to deep-sea diver: "Surface at once. Ship is sinking."

Advertisers must now confront the opposition of tranquilizers in suburbia. Suburbanites are so hopped up that the TV ad, quack and all, rolls off their backs like a duck. (Duck that "water" cliché!)

"Are You Too 'Well Adjusted' to Experience Joy?" runs an ad from Grove Press.

The New York Times on August 1, 1968, carried a full-page ad for Nation's Business: Happiness Is the Federal Government Doing a Study on Happiness. If "Violence" is substituted for "Happiness," the result is the same. Government, culture and business are now one.

At slow rates of change the maladjusted person is a local "character." At high speeds he is a neurotic menace. For the same reason the artist occupies the ivory tower in slow-changing society. He moves to the control tower in a rapidly changing world. He alone can see the present clearly enough to navigate.

16

Will the American woman destroy the cigar business?

"Have a cigar, lady."

And if you'll just stay away from the big ones, suggests the Cigar Institute of America, female cigar smoking is quite permissible.

But don't kid yourself, cigar makers are well aware of the unfriendly female attitude towards those big fat stogies.

"That's why the 'Should a gentleman offer a lady a Tiparillo?' campaign," says Philip L. Bondy, a senior vice president at General Cigar. "It wasn't to get women to smoke, but to get both sexes accustomed to the idea of men smoking cigars around women."

But, says Forbes, in trying to win female acceptance of cigars, the industry is also flirting with the destruction of an equally important marketing concept— the image of the cigar as a symbol of masculinity.

"A cigar asserts a virile personality," contends Dr. Ernest Dichter, a specialist in motivational research. "A cigar makes a man feel independent. That's good. Women, naturally, will resent this."

Resent it or not, cigar consumption is down, reports Forbes. Back in the Twenties the average American male contentedly smoked over 200 cigars per year. Over 10,000 cigar companies ministered to his tastes, and the after-dinner cigar, served in the drawing room with brandy, was the very symbol of contentment, success and refinement. Today, to the despair of the cigar industry, he only smokes half that number, says Forbes.

Can the industry hope for a rebirth in consumption? Should they try to get the war babies to smoke? Should they keep trying to win female acceptance? Maybe they should push cigar smoking as a big status symbol? Or what about more diversification into more consumer products?

You may not find out all the answers in Forbes. But you will find out all about other businesses. How they are run. How they think. How current trends affect them. And these are just a few of the reasons over half a million businessmen subscribe to Forbes.

Another big reason is the unique insight businessmen get into how top management people manage their businesses. Or don't manage them. And, as we've pointed out again and again, if good management isn't at the helm managing, your whole business could go up in smoke.

With or without the influence of the American female.

Forbes: capitalist tool

A RUNAWAY WORLD?

"A burning would is come to dance inane."*

When the entire world becomes accessible at these speeds, "travel" means getting to the airport.

Three times the population of Chicago leaves O'Hare Airport annually.

A car uses as much oxygen in 30 miles as 30,000 people use in one hour.

Studies show that the roofs of American homes are beginning to feel the stress of jet flights. The pollsters have not lost their cool. They won't look at the folks till they blow their roofs.

The present ad had a deadly aim. It voices the deadpan mutterings of a tribe of highly motivated somnambulists.

Possibly a supersonic blast will penetrate the barbiturate barriers of these so progressive designers and decision makers.

In Old Testament terms all extensions and amplifications of man dehumanized him, from Cain onward.

*Finnegans Wake, hereafter referred to as FW.

Traveling can take the fun out of going anyplace.

Hertz
We can help a little.

JAPAN AIRLINES

"The West shall shake the East awake, while yet ye have the night for morn." (FW)

"Won't you join me?"

Goodness Geishas Me!

The East goes outer with our old hardware as fast as we go on the inner cosmic trip of oriental fantasy with our new electric circuits and circuses. The West has "discovered" the I Ching and a concern with the processes of hidden environments.

"The foremost newspaper in Japan" beckons to the Western producer: "Your Japan market is the 'Mass Elite.'"

Japan Air Lines announces daily service to Europe.

Europe...a new way.

Let's face it, if you've been making frequent trips to Europe, you've probably become jaded by trans-atlantic air travel. Well, we're going to change that by offering a brand new service to Europe at 9:00 PM every evening. Our destinations? Paris, five times a week—London, twice a week. What makes this new flight so special? It's Japanese.

Come aboard and relax.

The first thing we do when you come aboard our new Europe flight is give you a steaming hot *oshibori* towel. Aahhh! That's better. Then we take your jacket and let you relax in a *happi* coat. Already, you begin to feel comfortable. But don't go to sleep. Not yet!

Bring your appetite.

You won't want to miss the Oriental delicacies, the Continental cuisine, the fine wines and liquors served aboard this Jet Courier flight. And you'll enjoy such subtle Japanese delights as warm *sake* served in a tiny porcelain cup. If you like, your hostess will even show you how to eat with chopsticks.

Fly as our honored guest.

Remember the feeling of being ignored or left alone when you really didn't want to be? It won't happen on Japan Air Lines. Your kimono-clad hostess has been trained since childhood in the art of pleasing guests. To enjoy her gracious service on our new 9:00 PM flight, stop by your travel agent or see us in the Rockefeller Center. Our reservations number is 581-8585. It's time you stopped being jaded on your way to (and from) Europe.

the worldwide airline of Japan ✈ JAL

Won't you join me?

PUSSYCAT

The cultural bias of communication manifests itself in unexpected ways. Natives use movie cameras as if the camera were a hand rather than an eye. They follow processes rather than taking shots.

The saturation of the educational scene with the old movie hardware reverses education from consuming to producing, just as the saturation of the environment by the mechanical means of travel reverses many of the dimensions of tourism. The tourist no longer looks at cultures. The "rubbernecker" has had it. He now has to "put on" the cultures he visits—food, language and clothing—all at once.

The motorcar, which began as a hybrid of the musket and the electric circuit, is an obsolete technology. (Early cars tried gunpowder as fuel.)

Paradoxically, the congestion created by the car marks the return of the pedestrian. The gun as capsulated energy ends in the plane, that is, "a speeding bullet." The car is as obsolete as a musket.

The plane ends the relation of wheel and road.

The hippie returns to primitive hiking.

"The prayer mat replaces the Cadillac."

The steamship and the railroad created the centralized metropolis. The motorcar dismembered it into suburbia. The jet plane simply by-passes it, leaving it to become a ghetto.

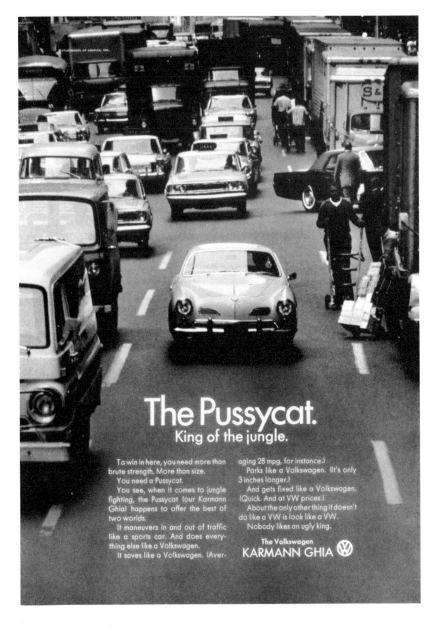

The Pussycat.
King of the jungle.

To win in here, you need more than brute strength. More than size.

You need a Pussycat.

You see, when it comes to jungle fighting, the Pussycat (our Karmann Ghia) happens to offer the best of two worlds.

It maneuvers in and out of traffic like a sports car. And does everything else like a Volkswagen.

It saves like a Volkswagen. (Averaging 28 mpg, for instance.)

Parks like a Volkswagen. (It's only 3 inches longer.)

And gets fixed like a Volkswagen. (Quick. And at VW prices.)

About the only other thing it doesn't do like a VW is look like a VW.

Nobody likes an ugly king.

The Volkswagen
KARMANN GHIA

TIRED OF
FEELING LIKE A COMMUTER?

Asked "Aren't you some kind of a communist?" Pierre Trudeau replied, "No, I'm a canoeist."

The airman who recently crossed the Atlantic in a six-foot sailboat makes Leif Ericson or Columbus look like a passenger on the Queen Elizabeth. He makes Lindbergh look like a BOAC passenger.

One of the many flips of our time is that the electric information environment returns man to the condition of the most primitive prober and hunter. Privacy invasion is now one of our biggest knowledge industries.

The hero of John Wain's The Smaller Sky tired of commuting. He noted that Paddington Station was a total service environment. He took up residence there with hilarious results.

"It is a democratic right of every citizen to sleep under railway bridges." (From the French)

A broke bloke in California recently refused $19,000 which he had inherited, lest it upset his way of life.

24

On TWA Blue Chip Service* to Chicago you'll get to know the hostesses.

Aren't you a little tired of feeling like a commuter?

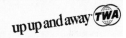

2

Breakdown As Breakthrough

When Jove had a migraine, it turned out to be Minerva.

HOSE-AND-LADDER DIVISION

War and violence result from breakdowns in conventional images of identity. "War is education." (War and Peace in the Global Village)

If somnambulism is a motivated state, the even briefer stay of stockings and light bulbs was a great discovery of planned obsolescence.

The hose-and-ladder division of the clothing industry creates even more consumer involvement and attention than the nearest fire. The hosiery gap cries out for closure. It is a fermenting interface of escalated change.

The black lady in the hosiery store asked for: "One pair of black stockings, flesh-colored."

A slip of the tongue gets more attention than an ordinary statement: thud and blunder.

All discoveries in art and science result from an accumulation of errors. Antisepsis was achieved in the late nineteenth century when anesthesia and the greater prevalence of surgery had created a mounting death rate.

Alexander Graham Bell, while trying to remove defects from the telegraph, discovered the telephone.

The New York garbage strike revealed the container corporations as the creators of the new American environment.

A Burlington Hosiery Product

When you've got a big fat run in your stocking, who notices anything else?

Infuriating, isn't it. If you'd been wearing Cameos, it might not have happened. Because Cameos are the slinky little 15 denier sheers that are knit with more stitches to the inch. The extra stitches give the fabric a fabulously silky richness. Yet help the stockings last at least a third longer than other sheers. Get them in all of fashion's favorite colors. For just 1.35. ***Get Cameos.***

TURN FOR THE WORSE

As any executive climbs up the echelons of the organization chart, his involvement in the organization becomes less and less.

At the top he is a dropout, like the head of a country.

Today, if anyone wishes to head a big organization, he must be "discovered" at the head of a small one. He cannot come up from inside. There are too many fragmented specialisms.

There are hundreds of American colleges and universities that cannot find a president.

On the other hand, thousands of high executives are wistfully wishing for teaching jobs in colleges. They could do a good "dubbing job" on the environments they have created.

I had just climbed up the water wheel, when things took a turn for the worse.

1 "You could hear it groaning a half mile away," writes Bill Tracey, a friend of Canadian Club. "Last summer, while touring the Near East, I came upon an ancient water wheel in Hama on the Orontes River. It reminded me of an old Ferris wheel back home, especially when I saw some local boys swinging around on it. I couldn't resist taking a ride.

2 "With the help of a friend, I got on. And as the wheel turned, I started climbing.

3 "As I neared the top, I stretched out my arms like a tight-rope artist balancing himself. Suddenly, the wheel stopped! I found myself high atop a swaying wheel, in the middle of nowhere. I panicked — and jumped!

4 "After drying off, I went with my friend for a relaxing game of backgammon and a drink of his favourite whisky and mine — Canadian Club." Why this whisky's universal popularity? Because no other whisky is so light and smooth and yet so satisfying. No other whisky tastes quite like it. You can stay with it all evening long — in short ones before dinner, in tall ones after. Enjoy Canadian Club, the world's lightest whisky, tonight.

Canadian Club
by Hiram Walker. "The Best In The House" in 87 lands.

BY APPOINTMENT
TO HER MAJESTY QUEEN ELIZABETH II
SUPPLIERS OF CANADIAN CLUB WHISKY
HIRAM WALKER & SONS LIMITED
WALKERVILLE, CANADA

A DISTINGUISHED PRODUCT OF HIRAM WALKER AND SONS LIMITED • DISTILLERS OF FINE WHISKIES FOR OVER 100 YEARS

ONE OF THE NICEST
THINGS ABOUT BEING BIG
IS THE LUXURY OF THINKING LITTLE

Nixon Cools Korean Violence. (Headline, April 17/69)

A big country can't afford to get angry with little countries.

News item: (Toronto Star, Dec. 2/68) "Widow with million in closet expresses joy in finding penny which she filed with note of circumstances, and deep satisfaction."

If psychoanalysis was the need for emotional adjustment resulting from accelerated social change, operation research forced creativity upon the entire business world because of the need to anticipate problems with solutions.

In Operation Research, as in creating a whodunit, you start with the solution and organize ignorance, not knowledge.

In O.R. teams, experts are excluded. They know it can't be done. In avant-garde art, as in modern ads, you start with the effect. The product that produces the effect comes later.

A Forsythe shirt ad shows a field of daisies. There is no sign or mention of shirts. You simply look and feel as fresh as a daisy.

By the way, "volk" is German for "cloud." The "folk" indicates a corporate tribal dream. Very good avant-garde art ad technique here!

They said it couldn't be done.
It couldn't.

We tried. Lord knows we tried. But no amount of pivoting or faking could squeeze the Philadelphia 76ers' Wilt Chamberlain into the front seat of a Volkswagen.

So if you're 7'1" tall like Wilt, our car is not for you.

But maybe you're a mere 6'7".

In that case, you'd be small enough to appreciate what a big thing we've made of the Volkswagen.

There's more headroom than you'd expect. (Over 37½" from seat to roof.)

And there's more legroom in front than you'd get in a limousine.

Because the engine's tucked over the rear wheels where it's out of the way (and where it can give the most traction).

You can put 2 medium-sized suitcases up front (where the engine isn't), and 3 fair-sized kids in the back seat. And you can sleep an enormous infant in back of the back seat.

Actually, there's only one part of a VW that you can't put much into: The gas tank.

But you can get about 29 miles per gallon out of it.

THE FRUSTRATED RADIO ANNOUNCER:
BLOWING BOTH HORNS OF HIS DILEMMA

"Shut up," he explained.

Confronted by the breakdown of the concert hall, Glenn Gould devised new dimensions of piano recording.

Confronted with the new electric environment of radio, the American Negro created jazz—an art form that integrated all the cultures of the world. The Establishment hasn't noticed this and goes on trying to "integrate" the Negro.

When radio became a twenty-four-hour environment, Muzak invented "programming"—unnoticeable sound adjusted to the hour of the day. Real groovy and tribal.

Announcers ignore the cool depths of tribal "programming" by shallow efforts to hot up and focus individual attention.

This dilemma is a breakdown that could yield large new discoveries if accepted as an opportunity and not a mere headache.

The most frustrated man in radio.

Life can be trying for a radio announcer at a continuous music station.

In a way, we sympathize.

Just think. They spend some of their best years learning to talk. And then we hardly let them get a word in.

Maybe we're being unfair.

Maybe we should let our announcers talk more. (They really have excellent voices.)

Maybe an extra commercial or two wouldn't be so bad after all. (It's more money in the bank.)

But our listeners would rather hear more Mantovani and Sinatra than more station breaks and weather reports.

So that's the way it's going to be.

It may be frustrating for our announcers. But it's the only way we can play more uninterrupted music than any other station.

Of course, we'll continue to sympathize with our announcers.

We're even thinking of buying them a special gift to show our appreciation.

A book of crossword puzzles.

WPAT 93 AM & FM
Between the news and the noise.

"ONE MAN'S MEDE
IS ANOTHER MAN'S PERSIAN"

Technologically, the copy of this ad pronounces a complete misunderstanding of the TV medium. The idea that the new picture should strive to be as clear as the old photo and movie ignores the basic fact of rear projection in TV.

Fordham University tests have shown that even movies presented by rear projection give more involving experiences than if by ordinary front projection.

The cathode-ray tube is an x-ray. The audience is involved in depth. The TV image is not a picture but an icon. The TV camera has no shutter.

Commercially, the principle of ignoring budgets when excellence is at stake is quite sound. The principle gets excellent statement in Antony Jay's Management and Machiavelli, where he says: "Economy does not need an actuary; it needs a visionary."

His example is that of Admiral Sir John Fisher, whose vision enabled him to increase naval power while drastically reducing naval budgets.

Sony introduces the television tape recorder for the home.

You can electronically record anything you see or hear, and
play it back instantly.
You can record and keep anything you see on your TV set.
You can erase the tape immediately and reuse it, or keep it
indefinitely.

SONY VIDEOCORDER

3.

Culture Is Our Business

A 20th Century-Fox executive in Paris arranged
for an exhibit of the fake paintings used in
the movie <u>How to Steal a Million</u>. He phoned
Howard Newman of the New York office,
who said the fakes could not be shipped
because they were on tour.

"What should I do?" asked the Paris man
    frantically.

"Get some originals," said Newman.
"Nobody'll know the difference."
(Sheilah Graham, <u>NANA</u>)

END OF THE "MUDDLE CRASS" AND THE SUGAR DADDIES

How can you tell if elephants are sleeping?

Today, night-club entertainers may often be hi-fi betas.

An IBM ad is headed: This Philosopher Wants Tomorrow's Students to Get the Best Teaching Possible—With or Without Computers. It continues, concerning its philosopher, Bruce Moncrieff: This Man Runs a "Finishing School" That Nobody Ever Finishes.

The computer salesman must return to school regularly to keep up.

Even as war is an accelerated and compulsory education program for friend and foe alike, so education today has become an all-out technological war on our culture and psyches.

The moving of information into psychic gaps and the "scrubbing" of old psychic programming have become the biggest business in the world. Hardware is incidental.

The budget for instruction (on company time) exceeds the total community education budget more than a dozen times.

The Armed Services include huge university staffs. As education is war so war is education, even as new technology creates the loss of identity that is violence.

One of the scandals of our age: Vast expenditure on "new" educational hardware of nineteen-century relevance.

40

American Can Company has a challenge for you:

Can you figure out how many mugs will balance the flower pot?
Here at American Can we have a similar problem…balancing people with jobs.
Because of our recent growth, a lot of exciting new jobs have been created.
Luckily we've got a lot of exciting people, too.
To help match the people with the jobs we've developed a unique team of managers who specialize in studying each employee's individual growth and development. To identify all the qualified candidates for each new job, this team uses a computerized records system.
Once we've identified all the qualified employees for a job, we're ready to start interviewing and selecting. Knowing that we haven't overlooked anyone.
This way we're almost always able to balance the right opportunity with the right person. Including the man who manages the computer!
Of course you don't need a computer to tell you that one ear of corn will balance ⅔ of a cat. Do you?

American Can Company
Creative products that
shape your future.
100 Park Avenue
New York, N.Y. 10017

AMERICAN
CAN COMPANY

GROW FOOD

"Never open me mouth but I puts my feed in it." (FW)

Tank farming is now done in skyscrapers.

In the information age, man lives not by bread alone but by slogans also. Food explosion masks population explosion. Bomb seen as threat to population explosion.

Love thy label as thyself (FW)

Werner Sombart is only one eminent economist who argued that historically food is the dynamic of all drive for change.

Culture and agriculture have been synonymous through most of human history.

First, the hunter, then the miner of the soil; next the mechanical industrialist. And now the information engineer.

The electric information environment returns all men to the condition of the hunter.

On the reverse side of ad shown was a woodpecker ad for Eaton Yale & Towne, Inc. Microelectronics: A Control System to "Peck" 800 Times a Second. The Idea Turned Us On.

Cain was the first plowman. He abandoned sheepherding for technology.

42

GROW FOOD

...feed hundreds from land one family starves on today.

Allied Chemical makes the nitrogen that makes food grow. Nitrogen fertilizers. They bring worn-out soil back to life—enrich it, too. And farms that once barely supported the farmer now produce food enough for even the farmer's customers. Imagine what this can do for the world's underdeveloped, undernourished countries. It's another example of how Allied puts chemistry to work.

ASK Allied Chemical

RIGHT IN THE CENTER OF
THINGS AT NO. 1 TIMES SQUARE.

Divisions: Agricultural, Fabricated Products, Fibers, Industrial Chemicals, International, Plastics, Semet-Solvay, Specialty Chemicals, Union Texas Petroleum, Allied Chemical Canada, Ltd.

T. S. ELIOT ON
"THE FRONTIER OF CRITICISM"

"I've gotta use words when I talk to you." (T. S. Eliot, Fragment of an Agon)

When an esoteric poet addresses 13,723 people in a sports stadium on a high-brow topic, is the title of the present book obvious?

Poets and artists live on frontiers. They have no feedback, only feedforward. They have no identities. They are probes.

Men on frontiers, whether of time or space, abandon their previous identities. Neighborhood gives identity. Frontiers snatch it away.

"Old men should be explorers." (T. S. Eliot, Four Quartets)

Hence, the man on the frontier is seeking a new identity. Violence and experiment are thus inevitable. Make it new.

Slang is linguistic violence on a psychic frontier.

"I'll tell the cockeyed world."
"You're putting me on."

The poet dislocates language into meaning. The artist smashes open the doors of perception.

What makes a newspaper great?

"PUT AWAY THE PEANUTS, JOE, ...TONIGHT'S GAME IS A POETRY LECTURE!"

T. S. Eliot probably is the only poet in history to face an audience of 13,723 in a cavernous sports arena.

The event: the third in the series of Gideon Seymour Memorial Lectures, presented by the University of Minnesota and sponsored by the Minneapolis Star and Tribune. The subject: a brilliant discourse on "The Frontier of Criticism," which earned for the 67-year-old Nobel Prize winner an ovation remindful of those that rattle the same Williams Arena rafters during a Big Ten basketball game.

The unlikely locale of the Eliot lecture was made necessary by the unprecedented demand for tickets to hear the scholarly sophisticate who authored "The Waste Land" and "The Cocktail Party." Requests for the free admission tickets snowed in from the far reaches of the 3⅓ state Upper Midwest area, far exceeding the capacity of the University's big Northrop auditorium—where only last autumn, 8,500 people jammed into three overflow auditoriums and several thousand more had to be turned away in the crush to hear the second Seymour lecturer, historian Arnold J. Toynbee, discuss "The New Opportunity for Historians." As with Toynbee, some of the Eliot audience came from more than 700 miles away.

The Gideon Seymour Memorial Lectures are designed to bring world leaders in contemporary thought to the University of Minnesota campus for the benefit of the whole community. The lecture series was established in honor of the late executive editor of the Minneapolis

Star and Tribune. The lectures are another manifestation of the continuing effort exerted by these newspapers to serve and advance the intellectual and cultural interests of their reader community, as well as being an appropriate recognition of the past contribution to that same effort by one of America's most highly regarded newspaper editors, Gideon Deming Seymour.

In a region famed for the intellectual vigor of its citizens, the challenge to newspapers is great. The effort to measure up to that challenge is always enriching and the response frequently spectacular.

Copr., 1956. The Minneapolis Star and Tribune Co.

Minneapolis
Star *and* Tribune
EVENING   MORNING & SUNDAY

625,000 SUNDAY · 495,000 DAILY
JOHN COWLES, President

8

PRINTERS' INK

FAKE VERMEER

"Phoney"—"as unreal as a telephone conversation." (1910 dictionary)

"I paint fakes all the time." (Picasso)

"I have painted 2000 pictures. 5000 of them are in the U.S.A." (Renoir)

In furs the genuine fake costs more than real fur. It wears better.

In art, the <u>genuine</u> fake, Rembrandt or Vermeer, is just as valid as the real thing because it provides the same new awareness or perception.

It is the art collector and auctioneer who anathematizes the fakes. Genuine fakes lower the market value of the big collections.

Art is new perception. New art opens new worlds for our recognition and nourishment.

Psychically, art is valuable only when new.

Commercially, new art is kooky and worthless.

The gap between the kooky and the commercially valuable is closing fast.

46

"SO I MAJORED IN ART..." But who needs the Mona Lisa to prove it? Cover your bed with a wow of a spread—color it plaid—with "Quadrangle", a dashing new bedspread by Bates! This bold brilliant blocked plaid will never—repeat, never—let you, or your décor down! And it's sale priced for campus and young home-makers everywhere.

Back-To-School Special: Double or twin (reg. $6.98) now $5.98 • Dorm or bunk (reg. $5.98) now $4.98 MATCHING DRAPERIES (66" WIDE X 63" LONG) NOW SALE-PRICED – $4.98 (REG. $5.98). ALL PRICES SLIGHTLY HIGHER IN WEST. MACHINE-WASHABLE. IN BLUE (ABOVE) AND COLORS SHOWN AT RIGHT. ©1963 BATES FABRICS, INC., 112 WEST 34TH STREET, NEW YORK 1, NEW YORK

TANGERINE   GREEN   RED

Bates

ALL BUT THOSE
FIRST FOUR NOTES

"Sheshell ebb music wayriver she flows."
(Joyce)

The lowercase copy at the bottom of this ad reads: "Maybe no one actually said this to Beethoven, but then he wasn't in the advertising business. In this business, it's a wise, creative supervisor...who knows when and when not to tinker with an ad, a commercial or an idea."

The cave art of Madison Avenue has been by far the most innovative and educative art form of the twentieth century.

Ads outclass the programmed features in magazine, press and TV.

Like the art in the Altamira caves, ads are not intended to be seen but to produce an <u>effect.</u> The cave paintings were carefully hidden. They were a magic form, intended to affect events at a distance. They were of corporate, not private, origin. So with ads.

They are not intended to be recognized as new art forms of our retribalized world. They are not a means of self-expression.

Maybe no one actually said this to Beethoven, but then he wasn't in the advertising business. In this business, it's a wise creative supervisor, or review board member, or client who knows when—and when not—to tinker with an ad, a commercial or an idea. We like to think that the ones we have are wise and that the advertising we produce proves it.

CAMPBELL-EWALD ADVERTISING
DETROIT • NEW YORK • CHICAGO • SAN FRANCISCO
LOS ANGELES • HOLLYWOOD • WASHINGTON • DALLAS
ATLANTA • DENVER • KANSAS CITY • CINCINNATI

4.

Political Gap

TV ended party politics in Europe and America.
It robs politics of issues as it robs business of
goals and education of specialism.

Leaders seek audiences. Emperors give
audiences.

The three-year-old standing up in his play pen
in front of the TV sees as much of the adult
world as anybody.

RUN FOR YOUR LIFE

Black Rangers Street Gang Demanding Share of Power in Chicago. (<u>N.Y. Times</u>, Aug. 3/68)

<u>TV Guide</u> for February 10, 1968, was headed: Can Television Elect Our Next President?

NBC and CBS could easily become the political "parties" of the future, just as the New York Central and the Pennsylvania railroads were once the political parties of the nineteenth century.

"It is NBC's celebrated devotion to saturation coverage which keeps CBS running doggedly alongside."

"ABC on the other hand—for reasons more fiscal than philosophic—has shucked all the gavel-to-gavel habit and hopes that its 90-minute nightly special will cover all the necessary ground without exasperating those among us with less tolerance for politicking." (<u>TV Guide</u>, Aug. 3/68)

TV means that the Vietnam war is the first to be fought on American soil. Parents can now see their sons killed in living color. All sons become ours on TV.

You can't have a hot election or a hot war when the audience has been cooled to the total participation point by TV. The experience is unbearable.

The hotted-up political conventions could be the death of American political life, all for lack of knowledge of the TV medium.

Democracy isn't wishful thinking.

Even though a lot of people like to think it is.
Like the 40 million who didn't vote in the last
election. This bothers us. Because we know
democracy is work. That's why we sponsor
nonpartisan, grass roots political courses for
our employees and their families at many
Western Electric plants.

We try to interest them in the workings of
government. We hold in-plant voter registration
for employees. Inform them of the issues. Urge
them to vote. Encourage them to take an active
role in their party and political life.

We've been pretty successful because a lot of
our people are voluntarily getting involved: they
check mailing lists, ring doorbells, work at the
polls. Some even get elected to office.

So as far as we're concerned, we'd say
democracy is working. And that's not wishful
thinking.

Western Electric
MANUFACTURING & SUPPLY UNIT OF THE BELL SYSTEM

AMERICA IS NOT YOURS

The great corporations are new tribal families. It was the tribal and feudal family form that was dissolved by "nationalism."

Feudalism was an emotional system of corporate loyalties tied to a shared image, like a primitive totem symbol. Feudalism melted before the impact of gunpowder and printing.

Such is the modern corporation.

The fragmented echelons of the organization chart have fused into a common image of group involvement, the new post-literate conglomerate.

Like the individualist "nation," the old forms of private business and wealth have merged into a vast tribalism under the impact of electric circuitry.

Ferdinand Lundberg is consulting the rear-view mirror only.

America is not yours.

It belongs to THE RICH AND THE SUPER-RICH.

Who REALLY owns this country?

Here, at last, is a carefully researched book that dares to give the answers — in names and with dollar amounts.

Three decades ago, Ferdinand Lundberg wrote a political and economic analysis that rocked the nation and became a classic even while it was used as a touchstone by the New Deal. It was called "America's Sixty Families."

In THE RICH AND THE SUPER-RICH you will learn, for example,

> How the thrifty multi-millionaire can make $19,939,652.39 a year AND PAY NO INCOME TAXES, while his chauffeur pays hundreds of tax dollars.

> How placing mighty fortunes in foundations magnifies the financial power of the super-wealthy families.

> How the United States Senate and House of Representatives bent their collective wisdom to writing a tax law for ONE MAN'S BENEFIT.

THE RICH AND THE SUPER-RICH covers a vast range of topics.

> Here is but a sampling:

> **WHY THE FORTUNE-BUILDERS SUCCEEDED**
> **THE SWEETEST-SMELLING REAL ESTATE EMPIRE**
> **THE ROCKEFELLER MONOLITH**
> **WHIRLING DERVISHES OF THE MASS MEDIA**
> **THE SAGA OF A. P. GIANNINI**
> **THE CANNIBALISTIC MERGERS**
> **CORPORATE RULES: GENTILES ONLY**
> **INSTITUTIONS OR PEOPLE**
> **THE GREAT GAME OF CAPITAL GAINS**
> **THE EXECUTIVE MYSTIQUE**
> **H. L. HUNT AND THE POLITICS OF OIL**
> **LOW INCOMES OF VITAL PERSONNEL**
> **SEVEN WILDCAT FOUNDATIONS**
> **THE DU PONT DYNASTY**
> **TAX SUPPORT FOR RICH CHILDREN**
> **POLITICAL SOURCES FOR NEW HOLDINGS**
> **UPPER-CLASS CRIME**
> **THE FORDS OF DEARBORN**
> **BOLSTERING EXECUTIVE EGOS**
> **CHARACTERISTICS OF THE SUPER-WEALTHY**

Although standard publishing practices today would dictate a price of $18 or $20 for a copy of this 820 page book, I consider THE RICH AND THE SUPER-RICH so important to America that we are offering the first two printings of 27,000 copies at a $10 price. These are available at local book shops today. They are expected to last no more than a few days. Thereafter the price will rise to $15. You are urged to secure your copy today.

Sincerely,

Lyle Stuart

Lyle Stuart

THE EMPEROR'S NEW CLOTHES

FDR on his two feet was a democratic leader who backed policies and sought backing.

FDR, the cripple, in his wheelchair was an emperor, a tribal chieftain, who created new environments. Like Uncle Sam, he wore the whole public as his mask. FDR used radio as the firing line in World War II.

Leaders seek audiences.
Emperors give audiences.

Western Electric is typical of the new corporate, tribal and imperial powers that create whole environments.

These are the Emperor's new clothes. They are invisible and immune to criticism, save by the Peter Pans.

If he'd have talked to us, we'd have leased him all he needed to get out of Russia fast.

We'd have gotten him out.

We lease everything in the line of transportation and storage equipment from railroad cars to airplanes to terminals.

In fact, we at GATX—you know us, the Tank Car people—have been making it easy for American business to move their products for the last seventy years.

Of course, we've learned a thing or two about transportation problems in our time.

Things like you're better off leasing your equipment rather than buying it. And there are several reasons why.

To begin with, when the lease runs out your responsibility runs out, too.

Another thing, we'll take care of all your service and maintenance problems.

Last but not least is your money. If you lease your equipment, you'll tie up less of your money.

Yet, with all these advantages, some people still haven't called General American Transportation Corporation.

If they don't soon, they could all meet their Waterloo.

GATX

ARE WE PUTTING OUT
OUR POLITICAL LANGUAGE AND QUITTING
THE PALEY O'LOGICAL SCENE?

The Lars Daly act of 1952 ended the access of political candidates to radio and television. From now on, these new media can give the electorate only news and ad glimpses of the office-seekers. The Lars Daly act means that the new media are allowed to process the public but not the candidates.

A New York Times piece for May 19, 1968, was headed: Intensity of Feelings Towards Presidential Candidates Is Lower Than in the Past, Gallup Poll Reports.

Naturally, TV has cooled the public while press and polls boil and bubble.

An editorial in The Times for August 1, 1968, begins: "Public opinion polls possess the fascination inherent in any attempt to read the future. But, in fact, they are a reasonably trustworthy guide only to the past."

Minus radio and TV debates, the press and the pollsters are having a field day.

They tend, for one thing, to ignore the new role of the **pre-voting** youngsters as makers of new political images.

The three-year-old standing up in his play pen in front of the TV sees as much of the adult world as anybody.

So–you think you speak their language?

1. "New Frontier" was which of these?
  a. book by Henry Wallace in 1932
  b. campaign theme of Alf Landon in 1936
  c. Kennedy theme in 1960

2. Match the coiner with the coined:
  a. alliance for progress
  b. arsenal of democracy
  c. nuclear proliferation

  1. René Betancourt
  2. Jean Monnet
  3. Adlai Stevenson

3. Match the phrase with the popularizer:
  a. government by crony
  b. backlash
  c. cold war
  d. egghead

  1. Alsops
  2. Krock
  3. Lippmann
  4. Evans and Novak

4. Match the phrase with the definition:
  a. strike a blow for freedom
  b. take him on the mountain top
  c. join the waxworks

  1. sit on a dais
  2. make a promise
  3. have a drink

5. Define:
  a. spellbinder   b. stem winder   c. sidewinder   d. high binder

See below for answers

If any one man knows all the answers, it's William Safire—
who was a key aide in the Nixon, Rockefeller, and Javits
campaigns. And if any one book can help you tell the ploys from
the platitudes, the stem winders from the high binders in this
election year, it's this one. Each of its 1,000 definitions is
accompanied by an informative, often amusing article. Here is a
comprehensive, fascinating guide to the way words are used in
political combat to inspire or inflame, to rally or destroy.
"FASCINATING, FUNNY AND ABOVE ALL, USEFUL."
—THEODORE H. WHITE

THE NEW LANGUAGE OF
POLITICS

AN ANECDOTAL DICTIONARY OF CATCHWORDS,
SLOGANS & POLITICAL USAGE

By WILLIAM SAFIRE

$10, now at your bookstore · RANDOM HOUSE

Answers: 1. All three **2.** As matched **3.** a-2, b-4, c-3, d-1 **4.** a-3, b-2, c-1 **5.** a. rousing speech b. rousing speech c. low blow d. influential but dishonest politician

LEAD KINDLY FOWL

Are You a Candidate for the Electorate Chair?

The New York Times, Washington, May 23, 1968: Senate, Voting Crime Bill, Backs Broad Wiretapping.

"From a jail came the wail of a down-hearted frail." (De Sylva, Brown, & Henderson)

"Why don't they leave us broads alone?"

"Wiretapping," quoth the raven, "is a threat to identity. Why not beat 'em to the wire? Get rid of your identity now."

TV puts the cool candidate in the voting-machine pressure cooker.

TV bypasses the ballot box as a means of creating political representatives. The politician can no longer "represent" anybody. He must become his admirers by turning himself into a new image of abstract art.

Art abandoned representation a century ago. "Matching" is a visual technique alien to the age of electric involvement and image-making.

In the cool TV age, the office must chase the man, as in the pre-railway days of Jefferson and Washington. Anyone <u>seeking</u> office is far too hot for the new cool electorate.

Television.
It's turned party politics into participation politics.

The Presidential campaigns, urban ghettos, racial violence, Vietnam —television thrusts people into the midst of what's happening. And their response, in turn, affects the nation's course.

Never has a society been so aware of global events. And never before have so many Americans been prepared to take a stand on national and international issues. In-depth, vivid, on-the-scene television coverage is largely responsible.

Throughout the coming months, television's instant news specials, regularly scheduled news reports and current event analyses will add insight into our primaries, conventions and elections—and significant events occurring throughout the world.

Other May highlights for the selective viewer follow.

Hallelujah, Leslie. Singer Leslie Uggams in a musical special with Robert Morse and Noel Harrison. Wednesday, May 1 (8:30-9:30 pm).

The Admirable Crichton. Hallmark Hall of Fame: Barrie's satire about an English family and their butler. Thursday, May 2 (8:30-10 pm).

We Won't Go. NBC News Special: the young men who refuse to enter military service. Friday, May 3 (10-11 pm).

Discovery. Monsters of the Ocean Deep; The Vanishing Wilderness; The Backyard People and the Big Top Crew; Spanish California. Sundays, May 5, 12, 19, 26 (11:30-12 Noon).

The 21st Century. Atomic Medicine; The Computer Revolution: Part I; The Computer Revolution: Part II; The Four-Day Week. Sundays, May 5, 12, 19, 26 (6:00-6:30 pm).

Ed Sullivan Special. Bing Crosby, Ethel Merman, Fred Waring, Robert Goulet celebrate Irving Berlin's 80th birthday. Sunday, May 5 (7:30-9 pm).

Somehow It Works. American Profile: a review of U.S. political campaign techniques. Friday, May 10 (10-11 pm).

Secrets. CBS Playhouse: Arthur Hill, Barbara Bel Geddes, Eileen Heckart, Katherine Bard and guest star Barry Nelson in Tad Mosel's original drama. Wednesday, May 15 (9:30-11 pm).

Man, Beast and the Land. A tour of the Serengeti Plains of Africa. Thursday, May 16 (7:30-8:30 pm).

Robert Scott and the Race to the South Pole. Saga of Western Man: expedition from Cape Evans to the Pole. Friday, May 17 (7:30-8:30 pm).

In the Name of God. Saga of Western Man: missionary life in the Micronesian Trust Territory and India. Monday, May 20 (10-11 pm).

Sharks. The Undersea World of Jacques-Yves Cousteau: the life patterns of the shark. Wednesday, May 22 (7:30-8:30 pm).

The Big Little World of Roman Vishniac. Study of the scientist-photographer of microscopic life. Friday, May 24 (7:30-8:30 pm).

A New Era in Medicine. Tomorrow's World: a study of advances in the war against disease. Friday, May 24 (10-11 pm).

The New York Philharmonic Young People's Concerts With Leonard Bernstein. Quiz Concert: How Musical Are You? Sunday, May 26 (4:30-5:30 pm).

The Candidate. CBS Reports: the problems of campaigning for political office, focusing on one local candidate. Tuesday, May 28 (10-11 pm).

Monday through Friday: The Today Show/Captain Kangaroo/Sunrise Semester/Summer Semester

Tuesdays: CBS News Hour/Who, What, When, Where, Why, with Harry Reasoner

Saturdays: Captain Kangaroo/ ABC's Wide World of Sports/ Frank McGee Saturday Report

Sundays: Sunrise Semester/Lamp Unto My Feet/Look Up and Live/ Bullwinkle/Camera Three/Face the Nation/Meet the Press/Discovery/ Catholic Hour/Issues and Answers/Race to the White House/ Animal Secrets/The War This Week/ Frank McGee Sunday Report/ G-E College Bowl/The 21st Century/ Wild Kingdom/Walt Disney's Wonderful World of Color

Note: This is, necessarily, a partial listing. Time (NYT), titles and casts of these national programs are subject to change. Please consult your station listings; check also for noteworthy local programs.

Television Information Office
745 Fifth Avenue, New York 10022

5.

Violence Is
the Quest for Identity

At seventy-three, Groucho Marx pities the
poor parent of the permissive era:
   "What you should do with kids is slug
   hell out of them when they're small. Explain
   to them what life is about, and if they
   don't obey, give them the cat-o'-nine-tails."
Groucho is merely anticipating what the TV
kids will do to theirs. When identity disappears
with technological innovation, <u>violence</u> is the
natural recourse.

DR. SPOCK'S SPOOKS—
YIPPEE-YAP!

Spock was the Pied Piper called in to get the habits out of the rats by turning the kids into cats.

Alternate version of Spock as Pied Piper in Hamlet style: Spock speaks to Tiny Tim: "I am thy father's spook. Your mom put a spoke in thy wheel."

Now is the first "software" generation. The TV youngsters are the first to be divorced from the old dominant hardware of books and machines. This generation was baby-sat by TV. They watched it from their play pens. Gray at three, they had seen the gamut of adult violence and confusion in every part of the world. At the age of six, confronted by the old schoolhouse hardware of texts and tests: See Dick run, See Jane jump, . . . it dropped out.

At school the micro-boppers face the same dilemma as the top executives. No involvement. Both the kid and the executive are victims of somnambulist decision-makers. This book endorses none of these changes. To describe these processes is neither endorsement nor prescription. Every man feels he has a right to defend his own ignorance even when it mucks up millions of lives. My hope is to snap somnambulists out of their highly motivated and destructive trances.

"Had to quit school to find out who I was." (TV Guide, May 11/68)

The heir to American business.

THE MILITARY GAP

"It's not the brave man that's dangerous. It's the cowards that scare me." (The Virginian, Owen Wister.)

Duelist, awaiting adversary at rendezvous, finally receives note from messenger: "Have been detained. Go ahead. Shoot."

"The Vietnam war results from the loss of identity of the U.S.A. as a business civilization." (Robert Theobold)

Every massive technological innovation creates new environments that destroy national and corporate images.

World War I was a railway war of centralism and encirclement. World War II was a radio war of decentralism. World War III is a guerrilla information war with no division between military and civilian participation.

The entire Western world is going East (tribal) and inward. The East is detribalizing—going West and outward. No such macroscopic revolution ever occurred before. All identity images, private and corporate, dissolve. Violent struggle to regain these images ensues.

The nuclear bomb is not hardware. It ends war as a means of international power play.

"Well, it is a little exaggerated. We're applying an $18,000,000 solution to a $2 problem. But still, one of the little mothers was firing at us." (American flier, Vietnam, 1968)

POWER CONTAINED

This Henry Moore statue commemorates the first controlled release of nuclear energy at the University of Chicago on December 2, 1942. When in place, it will be one of the major Moore sculptures in this country. It will also be one of the few works of art to commemorate a major scientific revolution.

In art, in science, in all areas of intellectual adventure — nothing is so powerful as an idea that has come of age. This statue presents such an idea: the intertwined themes of embryo, mushroom cloud, and skull containing the cathedral-like vaulting of human hope.

Ideas that have come of age are the life of a scholarly press. At the University of Chicago Press our explosive power is contained in the books and journals we publish.

THE RISE OF THE WEST
By William H. McNeill. Illus. 829 pp. $12.50

THE POLITICS OF MODERNIZATION
By David Apter. 481 pp. $7.50

A STUDY OF WAR
By Quincy Wright. Unabridged. 1637 pp. $20.00
Abridged. 465 pp. $7.50

THE RELEVANCE OF PHYSICS
By Stanley L. Jaki. 656 pp. $12.50

AN AMERICAN PRIMER
Edited by Daniel J. Boorstin. 1018 pp.
2 volume boxed set $14.95 until
December 31, 1966, thereafter $17.50

THE PLAY THEORY OF MASS COMMUNICATION
By William Stephenson. 383 pp. $5.00

THE SAVAGE MIND
By Claude Levi-Strauss. 312 pp. $5.95

75th Year

1891-1966

UNIVERSITY
OF CHICAGO
PRESS
Chicago and London
In Canada:
University of
Toronto Press

ALIS, ALAS,
SHE BROKE THE GLASS (FW)

When Alice went through the vanishing point of the visual world, breaking the hardware of the looking-glass world, she became involved in a series of rapid metamorphoses, not unrelated to her tears.

"Who am I, then? Tell me that first, and then, if I like being that person, I'll come up."

Lewis Carroll, a non-Euclidean mathematical professor, was the first to denote the dilemma of a print-oriented world in his fable.

Today the tears of Alice have been institutionalized at places like Esalen Institute (Big Sur, California). In the July 12, 1968, issue of Life, readers were taken to the big bathtub where, forgetting sex, age and identity, the orphans of Western print culture can "scrub" their old identities by having an epic sob session.

One of the nice things about being big is the luxury of thinking little

That means having the talent and resources to send people off to faraway places to dig up the great little number nobody else has. The way a specialty shop should.

Or taking a fling on a couple of crazy way out items made by some craftsy gal out in California. And not worry about losing your shirt.

And having enough good people around to do all those nice little things. Like getting your package wrapped pretty without tying up the whole staff. Offering charge privileges generous enough for a spring's worth of super clothes. Providing delivery on something you bought in the afternoon—the next day. Not two days hence.

On the other hand, it also means one can buy big. The complete collections of the famous and the soon-to-be-famous. So you can see the works without traipsing all over town-to catch a bit of this. A dollop of that.

To give you enormous freedom of choice. Without compromise. With satisfaction. In the intimacy of serene little salons.

The best of both worlds, you might say. Which we do say. About that big little place known as Saks Fifth Avenue.

THE GRADUATE
I.E., KIDS OF TWELVE AND UNDER

The planet is their little round schoolhouse.

SCHOOL SUSPENDS 53 IN HAIRLINE DISPUTE (N.Y. Times, January 30/68). (Anniversary of time when long-haired Charles I of England lost his head.)

A gap is an interface, an area of ferment and change. The gap between wheel and axle can seize up when grit gets in.

Fish know nothing of water. A New Yorker cartoon shows two fish getting ashore: "This is where the action is!"

The TV generation is swamped, stunned by its new environment of electric information. The Greek word for environment is "perivallo"— to hit from all sides.

Any sudden increase of wealth or power erases old identity. (I.e., pretended condition of Tareyton smoker: "Rather fight than switch.") Hence, the affluent kids lose identity first. The Blues goes with big loss of identity.

Pop song:
Every day I wake up
Then I start to break up
Every day I start out
Then I cry my heart out.

Identity is making, not matching. Struggle, not goal. Cf. The Loneliness of the Long Distance Runner.

JOSEPH E. LEVINE
PRESENTS
A
MIKE NICHOLS
LAWRENCE TURMAN
PRODUCTION

THE GRADUATE

AN AVCO EMBASSY FILM

STARRING
ANNE BANCROFT AND **DUSTIN HOFFMAN** · **KATHARINE ROSS**
SCREENPLAY BY
CALDER WILLINGHAM AND **BUCK HENRY**   SONGS BY **PAUL SIMON**
PERFORMED BY
SIMON AND **GARFUNKEL**   PRODUCED BY **LAWRENCE TURMAN**
DIRECTED BY
MIKE NICHOLS   AN AVCO EMBASSY RELEASE   TECHNICOLOR· PANAVISION

PSYCHOLOGICAL INTERROGATION

All preliterate societies are communist, just as they are tribal. They have never experienced nationalism, since that is one of the visual effects of phonetic literacy.

Vietnamese youngsters, when interrogated, say: ''I did not know what it was to have a native land, because I did not know what native land means.'' (<u>Look</u>, April 16/68, p. 38)

When they fail to "talk" under torture, they are given "psychological interrogation": "You want to die as a Vietcong hero, but don't be so hopeful. I'll tell you how you will die. Under an American truck without anyone knowing it. I will arrange the accident."

To the tribal man this accidentality breaks the corporate bond with his people. He knows no private identity and seeks none.

The TV generation is postliterate and retribalized. It seeks by violence to "scrub" the old private image and to merge in a new tribal identity like any corporation executive.

This Warner's ad faced the story of the young Vietnamese.

If nature didn't, Warner's will.

Our stretch-banded *Young Thing*™ bra will do it for $5. Our *Young Thing* girdle will do it for $9. Warners®
THE WARNACO GROUP

LOOK 4-16-68 **39**

6.

Goals Versus Images

Doris: You'll carry me off? To a cannibal
           isle?
Sweeney: I'll be the cannibal.
Doris: I'll be the missionary. I'll convert you!
Sweeney: I'll convert <u>you</u>! Into a stew. A nice
           little, white little, missionary stew.

—T. S. Eliot, <u>Fragment of an Agon</u>

WHORLED WITHOUT AIMED

"Willed without witting, whorled without aimed" (FW)

"Same Goal, Different Worlds" (Headline on feature about Mrs. Javits and Mrs. O'Dwyer, <u>New York Times</u>, July 31/68)

In our TV age, girls don't have the oneupmanship problem of goals. Girls don't have to specialize. They are all-embracing, as it were.

That is why there is still sense in G.K. Chesterton's remark: "Women refused to be dictated to, so they went out and became stenographers."

For the Man Who Hates the Thought of Being Average. The law of averages has gone over to serendipity with the computers.

Do you sometimes get the feeling that they named your car after the wrong animal, e.g., gnu or carsophagus?

Will Hix Buy Nix in TV Pix? (Anguished cry from GOP hotel room)

Careers today are for people who want more than just a job.

GILT FEELINGS

"Papa, what's a foundation?"

"It is an ingenious legal device whereby very wealthy families contrive to eat their cake and have it." (Ad for Lundberg's Rich and the Super-Rich)

"Here I am fifty-eight, and I still don't know what I'm going to do when I grow up." (Peter F. Drucker)

This Peter Panmanship is in the American grain: "The youth of America is their oldest tradition; it has been going on now for three hundred years." (Oscar Wilde)

The seven-year-old today has had a heavy dose of adult experiences and global imagery via TV. He enters grade school as an adult.

The increase of the human working span makes multiple careers mandatory today. "The older professions are best suited to become second careers. Middle age is really the best time to switch to being the lawyer, the teacher, the priest, the doctor and the social worker. Twenty years from now, we'll have few young men in these fields." (Peter F. Drucker)

The higher an executive gets inside any big organization, the sooner he drops out; because he has less and less to do with the operation.

Connoisseur, bon vivant, raconteur, patron of the arts, truck driver.

An After Six tuxedo can do nice things to a guy, whether he drives a truck or pushes a pencil.

It kind of makes him feel part of the upper crust. He goes to better restaurants. He tries expensive wines. Gets adventuresome with menus. Takes cabs instead of buses. Sees the biggest Broadway hits.

Why, under the influence of a tuxedo, men have even been known to open doors for their wives.

after
Six

OBSOLETE ON THE
DAY OF GRADUATION

Image making succeeds goal matching in a time when the targets change faster than the aims. At present, the day an engineer or a medical student graduates, he is obsolete.

The trouble with a cheap, specialized education is that you never stop paying for it.

In the age of the information hunter, feedback yields to feedforward, the point of view becomes the probe. Problems become discoveries.

As the information environment becomes a corporate teaching machine, adopting a college is like buying London Bridge or a Rembrandt.

Alarmed parent to son, accepted at university: "Columbia! But what'll the neighbors say?"

Daniel Boorstin in Image: Or, What Happened to the American Dream rehearses a mass of fascinating evidence for the disappearance of goals and direction in American life. (He deplores, but seeks no cause.)

MANAGEMENT MAN

Today, the majority of corporation executives are college-educated. Tomorrow, the demand will be even greater.

A college education is becoming increasingly important to the potential executive. It develops the kind of active, logical mind it takes to meet the challenging problems of the modern business world.

But the price of developing educated manpower is high, and getting higher. Colleges are finding it difficult to provide all the facilities that are necessary to maintain the highest educational standards.

If our colleges are to continue supplying American business with superior new talent . . . they need help. College is the best friend business has.

Support the college of your choice.

HELIX CULPA—RETURN OF ESP

In the sixteenth century religion went inward and private with Gutenberg hardware. Liturgy collapsed. Bureaucracy boomed. Today liturgy returns. Bureaucracy fades.

In the twentieth century religion has gone outward and liturgical with Marconi software.

"Any stigma's good enough to beat a dogma." (G. K. Chesterton)

Having called Vatican 69, De Gaulle inquired about the possibility of interment in the Holy Sepulchre. "Yes," was the reply, "for 100 million dollars." "What!" he queried, "for only three days?"

The present electric ESP age of multiple interfaces finds no problems in metamorphosis or transubstantiation such as baffled abced-minded culture of the sixteenth century and after.

In the age of religious hardware and fragmented lineality, it was obvious that since life was short, our faces should be long.

The
Religious
Situation

We're breaking all the rules in the book to bring you a totally new kind of book. This is the very first volume of what will be an *annual* evaluation of the worldwide role and status of religion in modern life. It is being written by some of the world's outstanding theologians, scientists, historians, philosophers, sociologists, anthropologists, journalists, literary critics, and other exciting contemporary thinkers. They discuss the religious implications of issues like LSD, black power, "the pill," Red China, electric technology, etc. You'll find it provocative, stimulating, scholarly, informative, and above all, *useful* ... 800 pages of fascinating ideas, imaginatively illustrated, clothbound, for $15. Offered for a limited time only at a 50% discount.

Among the Contributing Editors: Robert Bellah, Erik Erikson, Emil Fackenheim, Clifford Geertz, Milton Himmelfarb, Martin Marty, Michael Novak, Thomas O'Dea, Huston Smith, John Voss, *and many others.*

7.

(Hot/Cool) Groovy: Rut or Grave?

Men wanted for Hazardous Journey. Small wages, bitter cold, long months of complete darkness, constant danger, safe return doubtful. Honor and recognition in case of success. (Ernest Shackleton's original cool ad in the London <u>Times</u>. It had many takers.)

HOT FOOT

Commenting on the hotted-up gruel of the GOP Miami convention, Jack Gould noted: "...and now the question arises if television and politics can survive each other." (<u>N.Y. Times</u>, Aug. 9/68)

Why Are Buttons Better Than Billboards? Why is the story board at an Advertising Agency more involving than the finished ad? Why are ads better than the features on TV and in magazines?

Is There a Life Before Death? Stamp Out First Marriages! Correct English is hot. Slang is cool. No child ever made a verbal mistake in slang. He's too involved to get it wrong.

<u>The Lore and Language of School Children</u> by the Opies is a story of the complex and homogeneous culture of kids from Liverpool and Toronto to Melbourne and Belfast. It never changes.

"History as her is harped" (<u>FW</u>) is ineradicable. It is the written word that is hot, fashionable, transient and fluctuating.

The present ad is utterly antithetic to skiing. Skiing is involving, kinetic, cool. The ad hots it up. Fragments it. Is a flop.

Color TV is the coolest possible mythic medium. In the hands of the old movie gang, it is used for hot effects of more intense realism.

The TV sound track still yields the hot radio pitch, even in ads—a fatal error.

86

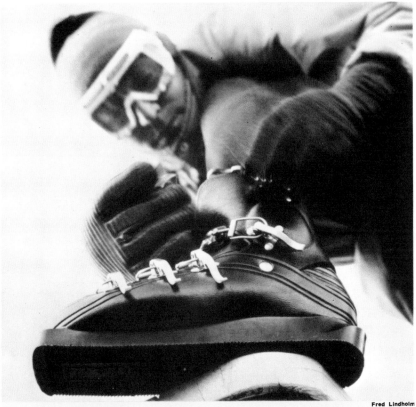

Fred Lindholm

HOT - FOOT

Some of the best skiing this season will be during those really cold days. Lange lets you stay outside where the action is,--not inside painfully thawing out ice cube toes.

LANGE BOOTS are warmer because of the materials we use. The outer shell has the exclusive Lange formulation of flexible-epoxi which actually resists the cold. It's seamless, waterproof, and maintenance free.

The inner boot has thousands of tiny holes in the padding which lets air circulate freely. Your feet are always warm and dry.

LANGE ski boots were designed for warmth and comfort, but that's only part of the story. The narrow sole (a ski width or less) gives you the ultimate in edge control. A non skid tread design is new this year, along with the contoured tongue and 180° Swivel/Post buckle system.

GET LANGE- - the ski boot that lets you stay where the action is.

WHEN THE TAG GOES ON

Photographic realism hotted up the reel world, while artists like Aubrey Beardsley were cooling it with abstraction and mosaics.

Abstract art is the art of making the image, not the art of matching inner and outer. Theme of E. H. Gombrich's <u>Art and Illusion</u>.

We Try Softer (The Electric Circus)

Roses at Belsen
Cantatas at Auschwitz

Death camp victims suddenly shifted into child roles, treating wardens as parents.

A Japanese wife never speaks irritably to her husband. She rearranges the flowers.

The only cool PR is provided by one's enemies. They toil incessantly and for free.

When the tag goes on, it will read

AVRIL

Hi-Performance rayon

Avril rayon makes the fashion statement of the times. It takes the long or the short of it. Styled with throwbacks to yesteryear or signs of things to come. And gives it the feeling of now. Carefree and comfy. Light and lively. Free. And eager to stand alone or make out as a great linen, crepe or knit. So go all the way. Break out in Avril high performance rayon. And let yourself fly.

Avril rayon, a product of American Viscose Division, FMC Corp., is made from highly purified and specialized grades of chemical cellulose produced by ITT Rayonier Incorporated, a subsidiary of International Telephone & Telegraph Corporation, New York, N.Y.

TEETH IN IT

A specimen of old hardware hot sell.

China Clippers Created New Frontiers.

Even osculating, movie style, is now unbearable on TV. On TV the hot screen kiss is the serpent's hiss.

Mr. Eliot cooled the tooth problem in <u>The Waste Land</u>:
"Now Albert's coming back, make yourself a bit smart.
He'll want to know what you done with that money he gave you
To get yourself some teeth. He did, I was there. You have
them all out, Lil, and get a nice set, He said, I swear,
I can't bear to look at you."

As Elias Canetti observes in <u>Crowds and Power</u>, seizing and incorporating begins in the mouth.

Our teeth are an order that threatens the chaotic world outside.

Smoothness and repetitive order, the attributes of teeth, enter into the very nature of the power structure.

"King Cadmus sowed the dragon's teeth (letters) and they sprang up armed men"; i.e., power at a distance, delegated organization, versus the armed horde.

Small reforms are the worst enemies of big reforms. (French saying)

90

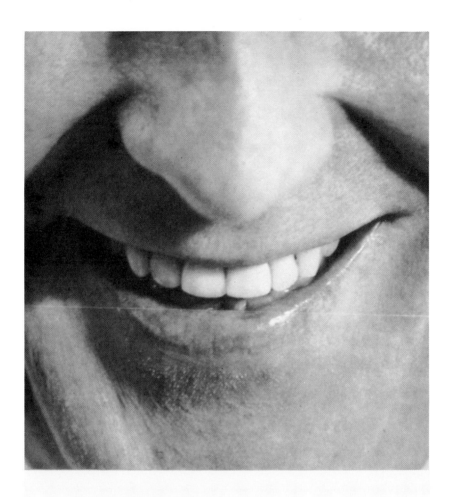

A winning smile
becomes a winning commercial
when the selling message
has teeth in it.

TARZAN'S LAST YELL:
WHO GREASED MY VINE?

Canetti in <u>Crowds and Power</u> pointed to the secret of the higher apes as identical with that of the stock marketeer. They could live in the trees because they knew when to let go.

Today anthropologists ridicule the nineteenth-century assumption that primitive man was violent. "The more civilization the more violence." (Ashley Montagu in <u>Culture</u>)

The eighteenth century had idealized the noble savage and Marx's rear-view vision saw communism as tribal.

The new industrial tycoon of the nineteenth century cast his image over the savage, hotting it up into a ferocious Darwinian grimace.

The Days of Cool Sport

Sport as cool and involving reached an all-time low in the 1967 football season, when the Dallas Cowboys played the Green Bay Packers in Green Bay. The temperature was 13 degrees below zero. The wind was 18 mph. The field was frozen. Bob Hayes, the fastest man in the world, made one 2-yard run. Many of the players were hospitalized afterwards for frostbite.

The original swinging society

Apes
have a very
low crime rate.
They pay no
taxes,
never go to
war,
never go into
debt.
They have no
population explosion
nor any threatened
food shortage.
No one has to spend
big ad dollars to
tell them, "Never put
bananas in the
refrigerator."
They don't need a
beautification program
because they don't
spoil their surroundings.
They don't pollute
their air;
don't waste
their water.
Their government is
a model of
efficiency and
simplicity.
True, they don't have
Scotch whisky, cellophane,
jet planes, ice cubes
or pro football, but
they *have* established a
balanced equilibrium
with their
natural environment.
A million years
ago,
an ape-like creature
came swinging out
of the trees and said,
"I'm going to
stand on two feet,
call myself Man,
and build a *better*
world."
Isn't it time
we got started?

Published with the hope it will remind some Americans of their
basic responsibilities. For reprints write: Director, Responsibility
Series, Newsweek, 444 Madison Avenue, New York, N. Y. 10022.

LET'S BURY THE HATCHET
IN THE SKULL OF OUR RIVAL

The age of hardware was hot.

The new age of electric software and information involves everybody in a single human family once more.

The old hot media of press and book still ineptly scream their messages at the new cool audience: "Make No Mistake! There is more book here than in a hundred ordinary books!"

The Rich and the Super-Rich by Ferdinand Lundberg is shaking up America! Gerald W. Johnson warns in The Chicago Sun Times: "Lundberg . . . is a positive danger to the establishment! He lays bare the guts of an issue that has been concealed under many layers of misrepresentation, mystification and sometimes downright lying. Thus he has produced a genuine rarity, a book with which you could stun a burglar, yet one that will hold the attention of an ordinarily literate man through all the hours it takes him to read it!"

Advertising needs both...

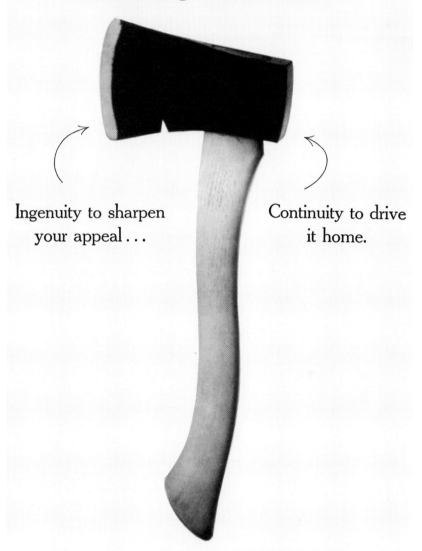

Ingenuity to sharpen
your appeal...

Continuity to drive
it home.

YOUNG & RUBICAM, INC.

8.

Centralism versus Decentralism

Albert in <u>Pogo</u> (July 27, 1967) says, "I'm going to start my own swamp!"

It is not only home and business that decentralize under electric conditions. Nations break up into older regional and tribal patterns. Ireland, Scotland, Wales are now strongly inclined to separate out.

IF YOUR SON RUNS AWAY
FROM HOME, HE'S PROBABLY
FOLLOWING IN YOUR FOOTSTEPS

Lenin was a naive victim of print-orientation. He could have bypassed the centralized nineteenth century and gone straight into the decentralized, electric twentieth century with his tribal and decentralized Mother Russia.

Albert Parry (N.Y. Times Magazine, Sept. 1/68) cites Stalin: "There is ground for just one party." Also Lenin's assurance that other parties "will exist in prison."

A Life ad reads: If Your Son Runs Away from Home, He's Probably Following in Your Footsteps.

The old centralized home, like centralized education and politics and the goal-oriented business world, was Oneupmanship all the way. Junior had to be better than Dad.

When goals disappeared, both private and corporate, with the total field of swiftly changing patterns of electric information, Junior knew he was licked. Dad had won.

Mom's fierce ambitions for Junior were a rear-view-mirror nightmare. He dropped out when the present hit him.

She's the spitting image of her father. She's even got his ulcers.

Some likeness! But she's not the only one who thinks Gelusil is baby food.

Many children suffer from ulcers. And if that shocks you, consider that your child could be developing malnutrition or hearing defects or heart disease.

Because ulcers are only one of the chronic illnesses that afflict children. It's a fact that one out of every five American children has a chronic illness and most parents aren't even aware of it.

What can you do? Know your child better. Emotionally _and_ medically. Take time to talk and play. A little girl's worries may be different from yours, but the reactions are often the same.

Chronic illnesses may often have very simple causes. Like an improper diet. But there's only one way to be sure. Take your child for a medical checkup at least once a year.

The more you take care of your child's health now, the less she'll need us later.

We believe there's more to good health than just paying bills.

Greater New York's
BLUE CROSS
Associated Hospital Service of N.Y

BLUE SHIELD
United Medical Service, Inc.

HOLMES AND
THE BUREAUCRAT

"Though he might have been more humble, there's no p'lice like Holmes."

Holmes, homes OHMS (<u>On His Majesty's Service</u>).

The cockney's "'omes" returns us to the oral tradition of the Beatles, the hunter, <u>The Loneliness of the Long Distance Runner</u> trying to probe and piece together a world that had been fragmented by the bureaucrats.

Holmes the probe, the artist, retracking the process of crime and cognition, is a creative being like Poe's Dupin.

Whodunits as process (not narrative) still hold up on TV.

Are you getting the protection you need?

The point is, security needs vary widely from business to business. A small plant in the suburbs does need a security force. Especially today when theft and vandalism are at an all time high. But usually not on the scale of a large industrial complex in a big city.

The big plant with extensive guard tours, employee and visitor control and dozens of gates requires a stable, dedicated guard force, relatively free of turnover, absenteeism and indifference.

These qualities are hard to find—unless you do the many little extra things Burns does to provide you with "premium" service. It will cost more. But you'll be surprised to learn that it may still cost less than hiring your own guard force. And you can let us do the worrying.

If your security needs are simple, you might not need premium guard service. But remember, last year American business lost over four billion dollars through theft. It might be a good time for a thorough reappraisal of your company's security program.

Take advantage of a Burns Security Analysis. We will follow it up with practical recommendations and costs—including suggestions for the latest electronic security devices, if they are needed. To find out whether you are getting the protection you need, fill out the coupon and mail it today.

NO BUSINESS IS AN ISLAND

"You don't need a degree to get in on this fine career opportunity in computer technology."

An ad for Loral Electronics Systems is headed: A Smaller Electronics Company Can Make a Good Engineer Look Better.

"You won't be off in a corner working on some minute part of a giant project. You'll be noticed."

This enforces my previous note on the need for big corporations to seek new heads in small businesses.

The Negro community has separated. Software in backward communities causes strong decentralist drives for autonomy.

The centralized star system in entertainment yields to the performer as mask that includes audience.

With all the field offices we have

you can build a great future just about anywhere.

You don't need a degree to get in on this fine career opportunity in computer technology. You do need a grasp of electronics and electromechanical fundamentals which might have been gained through such military training as: weapons control systems, radar, sonar, radio maintenance—and a strong ambition to build a real future.

Here's how we do it at UNIVAC. For one thing, we'll teach you all about computers. How they work, and why. How to install and maintain them. By the time you're finished with our training program you're a top notch, all round expert, fully equipped to handle any problems you'll encounter. And all the time you're learning you're on the payroll.

Now, when you're ready to show what you can do, we'll assign you to one of our field offices. With the kind of growth you'd expect from UNIVAC, you'll find them everywhere in the nation, and overseas. Covering a full range of assignments. Of course, you come in under our comprehensive benefits program. And with the way we reward technical ability and initiative, a good man can really go far.

Interested candidates are invited to write Manager of Field Administration, UNIVAC, P. O. Box 8100, Philadelphia, Pa.

UNIVAC
DIVISION OF SPERRY RAND CORPORATION

An Equal Opportunity Employer

TV: CRISIS VERSUS SERVICE

At present, TV is a service only during a crisis.

Surely, it is not unbelievable that decision-makers are totally out of touch with the world they live in? How could any contemporary person in any age be entrusted with powers carefully developed and monopolized by people from the previous time?

A Western Union ad in the <u>New York Times</u> for August 8, 1968, features a picture of the tribal ritual of the Republican National Convention at Miami Beach: This Week by Satellite the World Is at Miami Beach. It is the first convention televised live over both the Atlantic and the Pacific.

Note that the total decentralism of national participation is negated by the central control over the programming. That is why the drama shifts to the streets.

The media tycoons have a huge stake in old media by which they monopolize the new media.

The Rifle Association lobby has rifled and ruffled nothing compared to the TV lobby tied to the old movie and Madison Avenue hardware.

Subscription TV means audience participation in programming without benefit of ratings or sponsors. Instead of a package deal, the viewer will get service. Service as a matter of course and not a matter of crisis.

It's unbelievable.

After 17 years of mounting evidence
in favor of Subscription TV, would you believe that a powerful lobby
in Washington is urging a congressional committee
to deny you the right to choose.

Hundreds of editorials like this have been appearing
in leading newspapers all over America for the past year.

THE PLAIN DEALER

CLEVELAND   Ohio's Largest Newspaper   JULY 7, 1968

Delayed 17 Years

Subscription TV Is Still at Starting Gate

By William Hickey
Television-Radio Editor

WILLIAM
HICKEY

People throughout the country are marveling at the power of the National Rifle Association's lobby and its successful efforts to thwart the will of the majority of American people, as far as gun registration laws are concerned.

There is another lobby in Washington that makes the NRA's look strictly minor league. It is made up of movie theater owners and poobahs from the commercial television networks.

What have they done to rate such attention?

They have managed to squelch all attempts of the subscription television proponents to get their brainchild off the ground. They have managed this year after year since 1952, when pay TV backers first approached the Federal Communications Commission to authorize this service on a nation-wide scale.

For 17 years, subscription television advocates have been unsuccessful in advancing their cause, despite the fact that every argument against pay - TV has been turned into an absurdity.

To date there is exactly one subscription television station in the country, WHCT in Hartford, Conn. WHCT has been in operation since June 1963, transmitting a scrambled signal to viewers with special decoders attached to their television sets.

Those subscribing to WHCT pay an installation fee, a monthly rental fee and are billed additionally for whatever programs they watch.

One station after 17 years — whatever happened to the freedom of choice Americans were supposed to have? In a society where businesses make it solely on the law of supply and demand, the sub-

scription television people have not even been given the chance to fall on their face.

What makes the situation all the more incredible is that subscription television has the backing of the FCC, the government's regulatory agency for broadcasting, and the Supreme Court of The United States, which unanimously upheld the FCC's right to authorize the Hartford experiment.

Unbelievable?   That's exactly what is said by everyone who studies the situation.

Technically, there are no barriers to implementing a nation - wide subscription television system. Any number of UHF stations are available and most home receivers could be made adaptable.

Last year, in an attempt to persuade those aligned with movie theaters and commercial television networks, the FCC suggested that pay - TV be tried nationally on a limited basis. It also recommended a number of rules which would safeguard the interests of the existing commercial service.

Among the rules proposed

by the FCC governing pay-TV, the most significant were:

Only areas having at least four commercial television stations would be eligible to take part in the experiment and only one STV license would be granted in that area.

STV stations could not show a feature film more than two years old, nor broadcast a sports event that was regularly televised within the community in a preceeding period of two years. Also that the two (films and sports events) could not equal 90 per cent of the station's programming.

These rules would prevent direct competition between commercial and subscription television. In short, the present fare offered by commercial television would continue, but additional avenues of entertainment would be opened up by pay - TV.

It is true that educational television is attempting programming similar to that planned for pay - TV. However, educational television is seriously impeded by many things, the gravest of which is insufficient funding.

Subscription television could present Shakespeare opera, or what have you and the money would be there, collected from the viewers of the program. There would be no need to

wait for another Ford Foundation grant to plan future programming.

One of the most important facts to come from the FCC's study of the Hartford experiment was that lower and middle income families, who normally cannot afford the cost of live theater entertainment, comprised the majority of Hartford viewers. Hence, the theaters were losing nothing, but many people were enriched by pay - TV.

After 17 years, of frustrating and exhausting debate, it is time Congress unties the FCC's hands and gives the American public the right to either accept or reject subscription television.

Then and only then will I believe that politician who said, "The American people are the real owners of the airwaves."

Don't let this lobby take away your right to choose.
You, the public, should decide the merits of
Subscription TV in the marketplace.

GROWTH COUNTRY

The canyon in the image here consists of walls of printed stock quotations. The cowboys as stock men provide several visual puns.

The cowboy was created by the railway and canned tomatoes (and sardines) as Owen Wister explains early in <u>The Virginian</u>.

Our stock market was created by the telegraph and the telephone, and its panics are engineered by carefully orchestrated stories in the press.

Man's reach must exceed his grasp or what's a metaphor?

Growth Country is a country of the mind. Its main adjunct is Ulcer Gulch.

The future of literacy is secure as long as this kind of quotation is available for human consumption.

Napoleon said an army marched on its stomach. The cowboys marched on their cans.

If you plan to explore growth country...

get a professional guide.

When the average individual ventures into the growth area of investing, he runs the risk of losing his sense of direction. For those interested in exploring this financial terrain, we suggest the need for a professional guide.

Manufacturers Hanover is such a guide. Currently, we have fiscal responsibility for the management of funds having a value of more than six billion dollars—for individuals, families, educational and charitable foundations, corporations and others. To perform this task, the Bank maintains an investment organization equal to today's challenges.

At Manufacturers Hanover, your investment management account is handled by a single trust officer on a person-to-person basis. It is his job to bring to focus on your individual situation the research and management capabilities of this multi-billion-dollar organization.

Whether you want to pursue an aggressive investment policy or intend primarily to produce maximum income, your account manager uses an imaginative and creative approach to that task.

Isn't this the kind of *professional* yet *personal* organization you need to help you get what you want out of your investment program? Ask about our Investment Management service.

...it's good to have a great bank behind you

 MANUFACTURERS HANOVER TRUST

Personal Trust Division—350 Park Avenue, New York, N. Y. 10022 · Tel: 350-5244 (Area Code 212)

9.

The Pool of Space

Ortega y Gasset saw the handshake as on its deathbed. Since TV in the United States, people tend to seize both hands and buss one another.

TOUCH AS INTERVAL

"I Want to Hold Your Hand" (The Beatles, 1964).

"To the blind, all things are sudden." (Alex Leighton)

Visual space is a continuum. On the other hand (i.e., interval as explanation), acoustic space is a sphere without center or margin.

Tactile space is an interval. Hence, beat and rhythm. The Japanese refer to the tactile interval as "pool of space." (Dr. E. Hellersberg) Dali understands that TV is not visual space but tactile space. That is why he arranged for the images to appear on thumbs that were carefully separated. On his horizon (top right) is a bit of brain tissue indicating the extension of the central nervous system that is electricity.

Joyce devoted his tenth and last thunder in Finnegans Wake to TV, "the charge of the light barricade." The viewer is the screen (not the camera, as in a movie).

It is the interval whether in music or mosaic or in poetry that compels involvement until we become part of the situation.

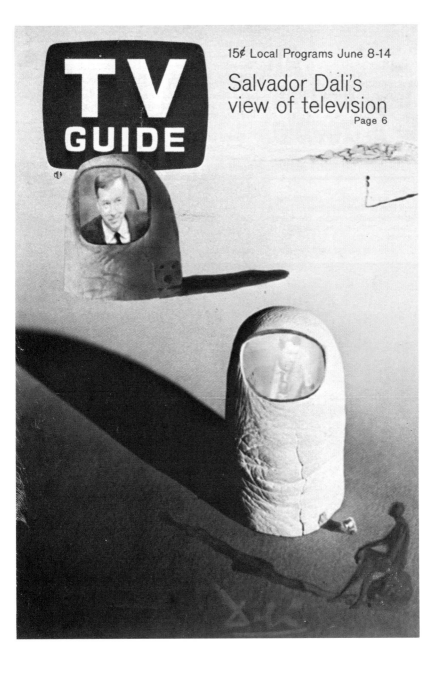

15¢ Local Programs June 8-14

Salvador Dali's
view of television
Page 6

KEEP IN TOUCH

The ancient seer was typically figured as blind. He lived by insight.

Ten cities contend for Homer dead
Through which the living Homer begged his bread.

Gap creates an interface or friction, and metamorphosis. Touch is Orphic. Upbeat and downbeat create intervals whose closure is rhythm.

Benjamin Franklin spun old playing cards against each other to create electricity.

In the electric age the connection in narrative and art is omitted, as in the telegraph press. There is no story line in modern art or news— just a date line. There is no past or future, just an inclusive present.

Thus, isolated news items are more interesting than editorials. Ads are more interesting than essay articles with their points of view continuously maintained.

Philosophic tradition has always accorded cognitive priority to touch among the senses.

Genetically, womb-wise touch is prior and may be the sense from which others became specialized variants.

Worship-by-Touch Services Held at Uppsala Meeting (<u>N.Y. Times</u>, July 24/68)

112

What could a blind Greek poet know?

Homer's blindness may have been a blessing. For the gods seem to have replaced his eyes with remarkable insight.

You can read his Odyssey and Iliad even today and learn why some men become heroes and others remain earthbound failures. Why some nations become great, while others fall apart.

These epic stories—which Homer first chanted 2,500 years ago along the shores of the Aegean—are the oldest known and perhaps the greatest writings of Western man.

Because Homer's timeless works so ideally represent the kind of books we offer our members, we'd like to send you The Iliad and The Odyssey, along with Sir Thomas More's Utopia.

You may have all three (regularly $10.17) for only $1, as your introduction to the Classics Club.

The Classics Club is quite unlike any other book club.

The Club does not offer best sellers that come and go. Instead, it offers its members a chance to stay young through great books that never grow old. Books such as Plato's Five Great Dialogues; The Complete Works of Shakespeare; Benjamin Franklin's Autobiography; Omar Khayyam's Rubaiyat; Walden, by Thoreau; and other fresh, spontaneous, even outspoken works that stretch your mind and sweep away the mental cobwebs that hold back most men.

You never have to buy any of these books. (To force you to buy a classic would be barbaric. As a member, take only those books you really want to own. And, you may cancel your membership at any time, without penalty or hurt feelings.

The selections themselves are remarkable values. They are carefully printed on expensive paper stock. They are hard-bound in matched sand-colored buckram, worked and stamped in crimson, black, and genuine gold.

Through direct-to-the-public distribution, we are able to offer our members these deluxe editions for only $3.39 each, plus shipping. (This low price will soon be increased. But if you mail the coupon now, you will enjoy the present price as long as you remain a member.)

Interested? Simply mail the coupon, without money, and we will send you the first three selections—The Iliad, The Odyssey, and Utopia —all three for only $1, plus shipping.

〜〜〜〜〜〜〜〜〜〜〜

Please enroll me as a trial member and send me the three beautiful Classics Club editions of THE ILIAD, THE ODYSSEY, and UTOPIA. I enclose no money in advance. Within a week of receiving them, I will either return them and owe nothing, or keep them and pay the introductory price of $1, plus shipping.

As a Classics Club member, I'll get word in advance of all future selections. For each volume I decide to keep, I will pay only $3.39 plus shipping. I may reject any volume before or after I receive it, and I may cancel my membership at any time. (Books shipped in U.S.A. only.)

Print Name _____ 8-NO

Address _____

City _____ State _____ Zip _____

The Classics Club

Roslyn, Long Island 11576

COME OUT FIGHTING!

"Life Is Fired at Us Point-Blank" (Ortega y Gasset)

Shake hands and come out fighting. (Referee)

The "missing link" created far more interest than all the chains and explanations of being.

Oriental art, like jiujitsu, is the art of the interval. In The Book of Tea we read: "In leaving something unsaid the beholder is given a chance to complete the idea and thus a great masterpiece irresistibly rivets your attention until you seem to become actually a part of it."

Holy Deadlock

Herbert Spencer's essay "On Salutations" is reviewed and assessed by Ortega y Gasset in Man and People. The act of the handshake has complex roots in savage rituals of hostility and triumph. Ortega y Gasset alludes to Dante's longing for salutation in Vita Nuova:
"I know very well that the lover delights in saluting his beloved; I remember that the whole of the Vita Nuova, and, as it says there, Dante's whole life, revolves around his longing for a salutation; I know very well that the lover takes fraudulent advantage of the occasion of the handshake to thrill with delight by causing the skin of his hand to feel the warmth from the skin of another hand. But this pleasure is not a pleasure of the salutation—which is no pleasure at all—but on the contrary is a fraud that we perpetrate on it, an abuse of that usage, the salutation. I do not know how it happens that love always displays a most fertile inspiration in fraud and behaves like a clever smuggler who never lets an opportunity slip. But the same lover is perfectly well aware that the salutation is no delight, since usually the delight of touching the beloved hand is purchased at the cost of having to squeeze several or many other hands, some of them annoyingly sweaty. For him, too, salutation is an operation that is performed perforce."

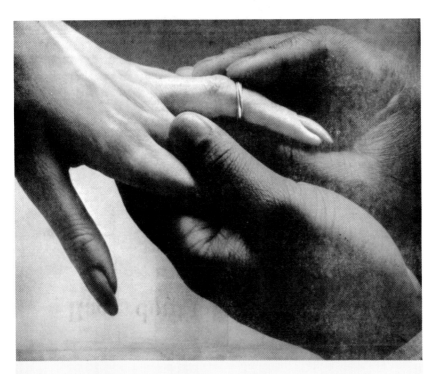

Races don't marry; people do.

Marshall and Sylvia Goodwin, Randolph and Marjorie
Wills, Walter and Jean Northrup, Arthur and Margaret
Levine, Kenneth and Marilyn Keane are 5 couples
out of 50,000 in the United States, who live it.

In the June McCall's, page 64, read the
headaches and joys these 5 couples are having. With
their families, with their friends, with our society.

Where else can so controversial a subject
be presented to women, as only women can understand. If there's something to be said on politics, on
fashion, on people, on food, on the future, you'll
find it in McCall's.

McCall's

First in circulation/First in advertising lines/First in advertising dollars

EDISON AND BRAILLE

Edison in his nineties, while his eyes were quite efficient, took Braille. It is a more involving experience.

The first typewriter that successfully typed was a "Chirographer" patented in 1843. It was known as "Thurber's Patent Printer" and was proposed as an aid for the blind.

Omar Khayyam Moore's talking typewriter is designed to expedite learning by involving all the senses at once in a mosaic like the Rubaiyat itself. It works.

The "literacy of the blind" is like that of the Chinese—multi-sensuous. The literacy of the sighted creates dissociated sensibility.

In music, up beat and down create quite different intervals and rhythms via "closure," Harold Schoenberg observes in The Great Conductors.

Duke Ellington at the keyboard.   olivetti's studio 45: the Brightwriter

BARE BONES

"This is your World Serious, 1969."

The Persecution of Leo Durocher and Assassination of Our National Pastime as Performed by the Inmates of the Astrodome in Houston Under the Programmed Direction of a McLuhanistic Wizard of Oz. (Chicago Tribune Magazine, Sept. 24/67)

Games are the mask of the crowd. Their dynamic is towards <u>increase</u>. They drive to <u>win</u>. Each nation's popular games project the image of its central dynamism.

Under a Bucky Dome a game becomes a seminar.

School is from <u>scholia</u>—leisure, play.

Today, again, after a period of classified consumption, learning in a comprehensive world is becoming play, pattern recognition, discovery.

Baseball may fade with TV just as football and soccer have increased. Baseball is one play at a time. Very little tactility. Much visuality.

No rules, no game; just rat race.

10.

Jung and Easily Freudened

Patent-leather shoes were verboten in 1900,
lest they mirror panties.

Sexually, man is the least privileged of
creatures, the holder of an unposted letter
"before the too late box of the general
postoffice of human life." (Ulysses)

LOWER THE AGE OF PUBERTY!

The epic of artificial aids for feminine allure is the Gerty McDowell episode of Joyce's <u>Ulysses</u>. If nothing could persuade the reader to scan the ad world as full of the figures of classical rhetoric, this could: "Gert's Crowning Glory Was Her Wealth of Wonderful Hair." The name of the Irish maid evokes the Scottish composer of In an (English) Country Garden, creating the subplots of non-verbal cliches that complement the coruscation of old verbal favorites.

Nature had not been kind to Gerty. She was lame. She made up the difference, as the present ad counsels. "Gerty Dressed Simply But with the Instinctive Taste of a Votary of Dame Fashion."

"Now Fatted Calf Is Out, Bosom Will Soon Follow" (Reuters, London, June 12/65)

IF NATURE DIDN'T, WARNER'S WILL

Is it all there? But in all the wrong places? Warner's® Young Thing™ bra will rearrange you. Warner's lace cups will make you firmer on the sides and fuller where you should be. Warner's stretch will hold you there, without squeeze. Warner's adjustable stretchstraps will let you lift yourself to your most provocative angle. All this bosom re-do in black, white, colors, $5.

Warner Slimwear—Lingerie. A division of The Warner Brothers Company

THE YOUNG THING BRA

THE HARNISHED BRIDE

"The Chemmy Circle" is the translation of Feydeau's French farce (1904) <u>La Main Passé</u>. The title refers to the then game of chemin de fer. The theme of the play is the use of a cylinder gramophone recorder concealed under the bed of an exuberant Molly Bloom type of wife. The recorded dialogues and monologues of her playboys make the play.

Feydeau sees the new hardware gimmickry as turning people into puppets, as Joyce did in <u>Ulysses</u>.

Ads have always insisted on the magical power of their product to turn people into omnipotent puppets like Feydeau's drunk who says "When I'm drunk . . . I'm bulletproof."

Tribal man has no awareness of <u>sex</u> in our fragmented sense. The pornograph came in the nineteenth century with the visual specialism of photograph.

My own book <u>The Mechanical Bride</u> records the effect of the hardware service environment on <u>sex</u>.

All has changed since TV. We are tribal again. Sex as classified positions of "morphyl man" and his <u>Psyche</u> has receded into the cultural past with Hugh Hefner's slippery blisses.

How to get your wife to fasten her Rover 2000  safety harness:

Tell her it drives men mad.

THE PAPAL PILL
FOR MECHANICAL BRIDES

"The greatest pill in the world today is the passion for the occult." (Denis de Rougemont, Love in the Western World)

Is it not a bit of eighteenth-century serendipity that The Fox should present Prudence and the Pill?

"Prudence, a rich ugly old maid, wooed by incapacity." (William Blake)

As machine hardware invaded the eighteenth-century psyche, Laurence Sterne, in his exposé of this farce in the first chapter of Tristam Shandy, has Mrs. Shandy interrupt coitus with an urgent, if untimely, question: "Pray, my dear, quoth my mother, have you not forgot to wind up the clock?"

"Some of my best friends are Jesuits but I wouldn't want my daughter to marry one."

Machiavelli with his accurate perception of the psychic significance of the new hardware (divide and rule) was regarded as a devil. His work merely implements the fact that the Gutenberg technique meant fragmentation and delegation of human relations.

Today, in the new software environment, an equally irrelevant identical response occurs in all "well-adjusted" people.

As a means of the mechanization of sex, the Pill elicits the loyalty of all those stunned by the new electric environment.

126

Alka-Seltzer. For People in Love.

You've all been there before. You know the feeling. You can't eat. You can't sleep. You can't think.

With Alka-Seltzer, though, you can weather the storm.

With Alka-Seltzer by your side, you can relieve a love-sick stomach, a tension headache, a foolish heartburn, and spring fever.

When it isn't even spring.

THE NATURAL
SUPERIORITY OF WOMEN

The Natural Superiority of Women (by Ashley Montagu) refers to their physical advantages.

Sexually, man is the least privileged of creatures, the holder of an unposted letter "before the too late box of the general postoffice of human life." (Ulysses)

Bloom meditates on Women, the Cloven Sex: "Ocularly woman's bivalve case is worse. Always open sesame. Why they fear vermin, creeping things."

After the death of Mrs. Johnson, with whom he had been very happy, Dr. Johnson was asked by Boswell whether there were another woman in the world with whom he could have been as happy. "Yes, sir. Forty thousand." Johnson knew marriage was not matching but making.

When mechanical industry separated home and work, women too became fragmented. Mechanical brides. Unmatched, mismatched, rematched.

In the electric age involvement begins again.

"... I wouldn't have believed that (The Boys in the Band), a play about homosexuals at a party, would prove one of the few good shows of the season ..." (New York magazine, Sept. 5/68)

128

This Monroe calculator has a memory like a woman's

…it can recall information even *you've* forgotten.

MONROE
A DIVISION OF LITTON INDUSTRIES

11.

"My Consumers, Are They Not My Producers?"

An actor puts on his audience as a poet puts on his language. A stripper puts on her audience as she takes off her clothes.

THE IMAGE: OR, WHAT HAPPENED TO THE AMERICAN DREAM?

Daniel Boorstin's book concerns the disappearance of the feeling of the open road as the American way of life.

The road is our major architectural form.

In an all-at-once world of jets and circuits, the open road has become the inner trip.

The idea of an outer world that should match our inner world is the visual book man's ideal.

An American Heritage ad for The Great West asks: "When History Is So Exciting, Why Settle for Make-Believe?"

The outer world has surpassed science fiction.

All knowing is making. All cognition is pseudo-event. All experience is a metamorphosing of reality. See Bartlett's Remembering. Scientific "proof" used to be repetition of an event.

When the Beatles had created their image, they returned to private life; "Records were broken everywhere, but to the Beatles themselves, it all became meaningless." (p. 203, The Beatles, Hunter Davies)

In English common law, as contrasted with American written law, the greater the truth, the greater the libel.

THIS ROAD WASN'T FIT FOR PIGS

That was some years ago.

Today it's a fine, safe Kansas farm-to-market highway.

California's roads are getting better, too. And Ohio's. And New York's. Everywhere, states are pushing planned programs of highway improvement.

Caterpillar Tractor Co., our client since 1928, is telling the country about it.

On-the-spot reports in general magazines point up progress in each state. And remind readers how much remains to be done.

Throughout the country, state officials and citizen groups both applaud this factual, positive approach. They've found that advertising, properly used, can help build roads.

N. W. AYER & SON, INC. | Philadelphia, New York, Chicago, Detroit
San Francisco, Hollywood, Boston, Honolulu

ARE YOU PUTTING US ON?

Glasses are now fun and games, masks, theater costume.

Dorothy Parker's quip "Men seldom make passes . . ." is dead.

"My Consumers, Are They Not My Producers?" (FW)

Young African writers today face the dilemma of having written and printed books in languages for which there are no readers at all.

The audience creates the author as much as the author creates the taste by which he is to be enjoyed.

The teen-age market was invented by the Beatles. In politics, as in war, youth is now a major factor. The TV set introduced the viewer as screen, the public as participant. It puts us on.

A century earlier, Baudelaire described the process in his envoi to his reader: Hypocrite lecteur mon semblable mon frere. The producer and the consumer make each other.

The process puts the public into total bondage to the sponsors and the programmers and their media.

ARE YOU PUTTING US ON

You should. You'll be prettier when you do.

And it's free! Come try on bright new eyes, dewy new lips, glowing new skin tone. Our Merle Norman studio artist designs this complimentary make-up just for you... to show how pricelessly pretty you can be!

Sound like fun? It is... at Merle Norman Cosmetics Studios everywhere. Just look us up in the phone book.

MERLE NORMAN COSMETICS

Franchise information write: Merle Norman Cosmetics, 9130 Bellanca, Los Angeles, Calif. 90045, Dept. M-1.

ZOO U.:
SURVIVAL THROUGH DESIGN

How They Make Hams out of Tigers. (Jack Paar even tried keeping a lion in his swimming pool.)

At the nation's most unusual college, four-legged students learn how to conquer many of life's obstacles. (TV Guide, June 22/68)

In non-visual space both man and animal are hunters.

Once a wild animal has experienced enclosed or visual space it can become visual, fragmented and docile like any literate being. It begins to regard its keepers as extensions of its own body; i.e., it becomes "friendly."

Ads like this one are intended to transform people into docile hams.

By topping the potential of hidden anxieties and aggressions people can become consumers like the hammerhead fish that feeds on coral and excretes 5½ tons of sand a year.

Those are pearls that were his eyes.

Such a conglomerate would not approach the pattern of business "conglomerates" as reviewed on Channel 13, August 13, 1968, by T. A. Wise of Fortune and James Ling of Ling-Temco-Vought, Inc. This meat-packing ham-wise enterprise has merged with airplane and computer productions. Hardware and software have kissed each other. The ham wot am.

How to make your husband smile in the morning

A. Lean over suddenly and rumple his hair. Tell him what a thrill it is to live with such a tiger.

B. Whisper in his ear that you've cancelled the new outfit you ordered. Tell him you have so much to be grateful for, you don't need anything else.

D. Tell him he works too hard and you're worried. Insist that he devote more of his weekends to golf and fishing.

C. Look deep into his eyes and sigh. Say you're so glad the children have his eyes. They'll be dynamite when they grow up.

E. Serve him pure Brazilian coffee. He'll dazzle you with his smile.

You've probably been drinking Brazilian coffee all your life. Almost every brand adds Brazilian beans for flavor and aroma.

But a pure, all-Brazilian coffee is another story.

Everything you like in a really good cup of coffee becomes richer and more concentrated in a pure, undiluted Brazilian coffee.

Unfortunately, unless you live either in California, Nevada, or Arizona, you can't buy a pure Brazilian coffee yet. But you can lobby with your friendly neighborhood grocer.

Tell him you want to try a pure Brazilian brand. And soon.

You'll need time to adjust to your husband with that great big smile on his face every morning.

COFFEE OF BRAZIL

DO IT YOURSELF!

Like all old gaps, the one between producer and consumer is closing. Production is more and more incidental to information. The factory depends upon it as much as the DNA particle. The consumer depends on symbolic data to direct his energies, too. Ideas have become the main ingredient of the new economy.

Consumer's Guide, given away in 1897, is a rare volume that is to be issued as an expensive cultural item in 1968.

The dangers of do-it-yourself appear in this item from the Toronto Star, Jan. 24, 1966: Dies in Home-Made Electric Chair. A technical student who scored 93 in electricity died in his own electric chair. . . . His landlord thought he was wiring the building.

The ordinary new pattern is: They Grow Their Own Play (piece by Walter Kerr on The Concept, N.Y. Times, June 2/68). When the Listener Is Composer (Theodore Strongin, N.Y. Times, June 13/68). Television as Participant Recorder (Harry A. Wilmer, apropos the wide use of TV and movies made by mental patients for self-therapy).

Audience awareness and participation in turn brings revolt against the offerings of stage and shop: Change in Average Housewife Brings Problems for Unilever (Toronto Globe, May 16/68); or, He Used to Enjoy Himself at the Theater But Now He Knows Better. (New York magazine, July 15/68)

This ad was dictated by the client:

**Tear it out and save it.
Your client may see it, too.**

HOW WE LOST THE WAR

War is a non-stop brainstorming session productive of many scientific breakthroughs. (Ramparts, July 15/68)

The theme of the Ramparts essay is quite simply the natural adherence of American military forces to producer-consumer patterns of rigid central organization borrowed from the home economy. Large central reserves are distributed to the enemy gratis. The oriental has no habit of centralism and every soldier is a production plant.

David Hoag explains how the British finally broke out of the lineal pattern of war organization in World War II. (Explorations, Something Else Press, N.Y., 1967)

War and Peace in the Global Village (Bantam and McGraw-Hill, 1968) is devoted to War as Education and Education as War. All technological changes result in war.

The Report from Iron Mountain, edited by Leonard C. Lewin (Dial Press, 1967), indicates the basic need of war in the Western world with "war-readiness as the dominant force in our societies."

The "non-military utility of war" in the economy finds its "most familiar example" in the effect of "peace threats" on the stock market.

Apropos ad: Can some recall the World War I phrase, "Lest We Forget"?

We work
like elephants.

For peanuts.

Dividend checks. Rights. Calls. Coupons. Tax records. Securities to keep safe. Conversion privileges to keep track of. Details. Details. Details.

What man or woman of means doesn't have more than enough portfolio problems like these to solve? (And never enough time to do them justice.) So why do it? Get an elephant like us. Then just sit back and watch us go to work.

We'll take all the custodial burdens off your shoulders. We'll guard your portfolio, collect its income, buy things, sell things—just as you direct (elephants are very obedient). And then, each month, like clockwork, (elephants never forget) we'll give you a complete run-down on the details.

It's a service we call Securities Safekeeping and Servicing. And the cost—much of which is tax deductible—is like peanuts compared to the mass of duties performed.

Right now we watch over tens of billions of dollars. Still, there are lots of people who need our help, and don't know it. Almost anyone with a portfolio worth $50,000 or more: Busy executives, people overseas, widows, trustees for charities, retired businessmen, doctors, lawyers.

For people like these, our hardnosed professionals can be part financial encyclopedia, part bookkeeper, part private secretary, part old-friend-of-the-family. (And loyal, like elephants should be.)

To learn what a few peanuts can do for you, write: First National City Bank, 399 Park Avenue, New York, N.Y. 10022. Or phone: (212) 559-6009.

It could be like getting your own elephant.

FIRST NATIONAL CITY BANK
TRUST & INVESTMENT DIVISION

12.

Sound Profile

The deaf hate reading and like math; the blind
love reading and hate math.

VERBIVOCOVISUAL

Most Disc Jockeys Are Paid to Talk: Ours Are Paid to Listen. (WPAT, Between the News and the Noise)

Ear-injury reports stir rock-music community. (N.Y. Times, Aug. 21/68)

Give the Gift of the Gab. (Telephone ad urging extensions for teen-agers)

American politicians are caught in the clash between written and oral traditions. Most political "corruption" in America results from the unconscious interface of eye and ear structures, e.g., the written Constitution versus the tribal machine bosses, the legal contract of the tribal mob of Cosa Nostra variety, the corporate and bureaucratic responsibility of members of Congress versus their private business lives. (See The Case against Congress by Pearson and Anderson or "The Congressman and the Hoodlum," Life, Aug. 9/68.)

The business community, too, is caught in the same clash, as William Whyte indicates in his Organization Man, which records the executive trauma of shifting from written to oral modes.

The British don't escape either. Arthur Bryant's Turn of the Tide records the oral-aural aristocratic temper of Churchill as it encountered the Civil Service bureaucrats in and out of the army.
General Alanbrooke: "...he shook his fist in my face, saying, 'I do not want any of your long-term projects....' I told him he must know where he was going, to which he replied he did not want to know."

144

We separate the men from the noise

1968 is already the swingingest Presidential year in history. There have been enough switches for a dozen elections ...and a lot more is going to happen before November 5th.

It's a campaign of statements, counterstatements, feints and surprises. You could spend 24 hours a day figuring out "*what they meant by that.*" But to save you time and keep you up to date the New York Daily News has a team of 16 seasoned political reporters to figure it out for you ... clearly, concisely and daily.

The News political team ranks with the best in the country. They *have* to be tops, because five million people depend on us for the news and the news inside the news ... reported in no-nonsense, understandable terms. Each of our pros is an expert in his field, whether it's telling the behind-the-scenes Washington story, taking the pulse in the primary states, traveling with the candidates, or analyzing the pre-convention maneuvering of the favorites, the underdogs, the dark horses.

Campaigns are known for oratory and hoopla. We're known for separating the men from the noise.

DAILY ⬛ NEWS
NEW YORK'S PICTURE NEWSPAPER

HERE'S OUR LINE-UP: IN AND OUT OF WASHINGTON: Ted Lewis/Jerry Greene/William Umstead/Paul Healy/Stan Carter/Richard McGowan/David Breasted Judith Axler/Ann Wood. IN AND OUT OF NEW YORK: James Desmond/Richard Mathieu/Gene Spagnoli/Edward O'Neill/Tom Poster/Owen Fitzgerald/Alfred Miele.

RED TAPE VS. SOUND TAPE

"With the sense of sight, the idea communicates the emotion, whereas with sound, the emotion communicates the idea, which is more direct and therefore more powerful." (Dialogues of Alfred North Whitehead)

The New York Times for August 5, 1968, carried the story of audio-tape wizard Tony Schwartz, who made the famous New York 19 sound portrait of a city. The article is headed Sound Profile of 86th St. Is Taped. Beside this story is another, headed: Jazz Harp Silenced by Soviet Red Tape. International strings were being pulled yesterday in an effort to secure the release of an American musician's harp. . . . Daphne Hellman . . . could not pluck it from the grip of Soviet bureaucracy.

All language is layered with puns that the penman (eye) suppresses.

The newspaper mosaic is crammed daily with visual puns of this kind. The mere juxtaposition of items without connection, save by dateline, makes the press a huge time harp of poésie concrète.

Long ago Mallarmé made a newspaper poem called Un Coup de Dès (One Throw of the Dice), using the spread-out sheets of the paper as poetic wings.

Finnegans Wake is "this allnights newsery reel" with a sound track, i.e., The Thousand and One Nights of Sheherazade.

Lawyer Sues over Wedding Photos—"so grotesque and repulsive they got him in trouble with in-laws and hurt his practice." (N.Y. Times, Jan. 30/68)

146

mommy, can I hear
my daddy's voice again?

A tape recorder is a distant voice brought near. Or capturing forever the thrill of your parents' Golden Wedding anniversary. ✂ It is eight straight hours of rock n' roll when your daughter's Sweet Sixteen. Or a talking notebook for a pre-med student headed for the Dean's list. ✂ It is a chance for Dad to prepare an important business presentation. Record a Beethoven concert right off the radio. Or your child speaking for the very first time. ✂ Because your life is so full of once-in-a-lifetime moments, our life is building the best tape recorder in the world. And the most popular. ✂ How many ways are there to use a tape recorder? Use your imagination...then use Sony.

You never heard it so good. **SONY** **SUPERSCOPE** ®

THE CODEBREAKERS

Shun the Punman

The East-West culture gap reached a peak with the Pueblo episode, when a band of yokels captured an intelligence center of the U.S. Navy. This is a "capsule" episode affording a mosaic glimpse of our age.

Cracking the code of our own popular culture is much harder than the problem of the Rosetta Stone image.

Edmund Leach in his A Runaway World? points out that "If we had different senses—more sensitive noses and ears, for example . . . our environment would not only seem different, it would be different, even though the 'things' in it were just the same as they are now."

He is mistaken in thinking that "if all man-made machines are simply an extension of man, they cannot constitute a threat." This is the folly of Alan Watts in his approach to human identity: "Society is our extended mind and body." (The Book, Pantheon Books, New York, 1966)

Both Leach and Watts are extreme types of the visually oriented. It is the naive visual man who falls into the oral and oriental trap, e.g., E. M. Forster and D. H. Lawrence. The visual man is a matcher, not a maker (cf. E. H. Gombrich's Art and Illusion). These visually specialized men can't recognize the metamorphosis of human identity that occurs with each technological extension.

ROSETTA STONE — A piece of black basalt found in 1799
near the Rosetta mouth of the Nile, bearing a bilingual
description in hieroglyphics and Greek. This gave the
first clue toward deciphering Egyptian hieroglyphics.
Photograph courtesy of Field Museum of Natural History

WE HELP KEEP IT SIMPLE!

Hieroglyphics belong in a museum, not in specifications for a temperature
control system. We feel a 'spec' should be written simply and clearly to
permit true competitive bidding. When Powers helps with a specification,
the system is described in straightforward terms, without restrictive ref-
erences to catalog numbers or obscure product features.

OUR 75th YEAR

Manufacturers of temperature control, water mixing, industrial process, and pneumatic despatch systems.

THE POWERS REGULATOR COMPANY OF CANADA, LIMITED

Dept. 7U   15 Torbarrie Rd., Downsview, Ontario

16-110-C

For further information circle No. 14 on Readers' Service Card

SHOT HER
ON MY AFRICAN TRIP!

Time Was a Really Good Movie Camera Sat
You Back a Week's Pay. (Kodak ad)

Dickens uses the pen as a camera with a child's vision.

Children or natives use a movie camera as extensions of their hands, not their eyes. The effect is utterly involving, like rear-projection.

(The Iroquois in high steel have no qualms since they don't have the habit of visual perspective. If you never <u>think</u> to look down, a twelve-inch girder high above the street is as secure as a sidewalk.)

Natives do not experience visual space; i.e., space that is uniform, continuous and connected. When given movie cameras to record their rituals and crafts, the results are quite upsetting to the visually oriented anthropologists.

Children love to make movies of processes: A feather floating to the ground. A man going into a phone booth to dial.

Shot her on my African trip, old boy!

Remember the tour I did of the Congo, Nigeria and South Africa a couple of months back? Fact-finding mission, they called it. Found out a lot of things along the route, by flying Sabena all the way. I've never been looked after so well as in those long-distance Boeing flights; they think of everything: English-speaking staff everywhere ... and the cabin service: really, you feel like a post graduate examiner testing the staff for promotion. This was my stewardess on the trip back to Brussels ... never found out her name, dash it!

EXPERIENCE SABENA SERVICE

BELGIAN *World* AIRLINES

FLYING YOURSELF—OR FLYING YOUR FREIGHT ...

BOOK THROUGH YOUR APPOINTED AGENT

Sabena regional offices:

LONDON GER 6960 MANCHESTER DEA 6956
BIRMINGHAM MID 6105 GLASGOW CIT 6018
DUBLIN 73440 SHANNON 240

SEATED ONE DAY
AT THE TYPEWRITER

We've Changed Our Name Because of the Sound. We Aren't Howe Sound Company Any More: We're the Howmet Corporation.

In the new software information environment sound images are back as magical forces for channeling perception.

Hospitals still use a maddening, monotonous, uniform hiss in their air-conditioning. A systole-diastole rhythm would be therapeutic.

Skinny Sony. Fat Sound. The Sony 6F-21 W.

Mohawk Airlines Introduces the "Consecutive Executive" Fare.

It was an easy step from the typewriter to the talking typewriter since the tactility and kinesics of typing is close to the piano keyboard.

The new telephone touch-tone system shifts from the merely visual lineality of the old dial.

The strange dynamics of the encounter of eyes versus ear are recorded in the Humpty-Dumpty story. The integral egg was not compatible with the wall. The civil service couldn't patch him up.

The Old Testament is against technology from Cain on.

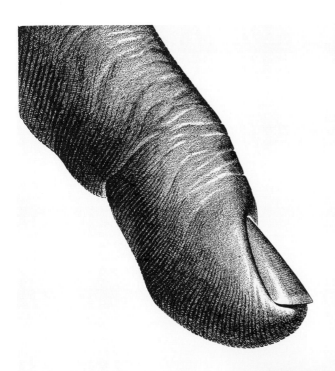

To reach
the men who
build America...

A 40-man editorial staff in New York, editors in major cities from coast to coast, 160 special reporters and correspondents throughout the world, the industrial news-gathering chain of McGraw-Hill bureaus and correspondents, 3 major wire services . . . plus contributions by outside experts . . . all this is why 77,000 construction men — the men who build America — depend on Engineering News-Record every week.

13.

Speak, That I May See You

Witness: "No, I didn't actually <u>see</u> him bite off
the guy's ear."
Judge: "What are you presuming to give
evidence about?"
Witness: "I saw him spit it out."

SQUEAK, THAT I MAY SEE YOU

"We'll Get You to the Taj Mahal on Time." (Beyond the Fringe)

"When I walk on Eighth Avenue, man, I see rhythms. I don't see downtown." (Cab Calloway)

The difference between a cliché and an archetype is the difference between eye and ear, between waking and dreaming. The space created by the eye is uniform, continuous and connected. The space created by the ear and all the other senses is discontinuous—without centers or margins. There is no point of view from which to observe sculpture.

The appeal of Freud to the literati can be understood via his visual bias: Emil Ludwig's Doctor Freud notes his absence of interest in the world of nature and his refusal over six decades of practice to consider even the possibility of music as therapy for bad nerves.

"Twenty-three miles from Agra in India, with its fabled Taj Mahal, lies Fatehpur Sikri, a dream city built in sandstone the colors of the dying sunset....Wherever the eye turns the view is held, but at every step it changes." (Jacqueline Tyrwhitt, "The Moving Eye," in Explorations in Communications, edited by Carpenter and McLuhan, Beacon Press)

156

TROUT AND FLY: Crystal trout rising to a fly of 18 karat gold · Designed by James Houston · Height 9½″ · $625

STEUBEN GLASS
FIFTH AVENUE AT 56th STREET · NEW YORK · N.Y. 10022

THE LANGUAGE OF GESTURE

"Gestapose to parry off cheekars or frankfurters on the odor." (FW)

This theme is explored in Through the Vanishing Point: Space in Poetry and Painting.

It was the anthropologist Bronislaw Malinowski who popularized the theme of "phatic communion" or language as gesture, enabling Mr. Eliot to put in the mouth of his caveman Sweeney: "I've gotta use words when I talk to you."

The whole of the 1920s reveled in bottom-wagging (the Twenties manifested "The Black Bottom," the Sixties the white bottom) and glorified the caveman idea. Cf. the Beatles' "Stone Age Haircut."

"Speak, That I May See Thee" was a popular aphorism of the ancient world. It is the title of a book by Harold Stahmer on the religious significance of language. (Macmillan, New York, 1968)

That Stahmer should make the gesture of such a book!

A tapeworm as long as a football field can exist in a movie star without being noticed.

If you are positively thigh-catching in pants

Ask about Lycra.®

You can look positively ah-inspiring in pants if you **wear the** right girdle made with "Lycra" underneath them. Girdles made with "Lycra" can whittle and make little of much. Foundations made with Lycra* **spandex** can slim you down, shape you up, nip you in. And keep you **under comfortable** control...no matter what your weight or figure. In short, nothing does all the things "Lycra" does! Ask for it next time you go bra and girdle buying.

*Du Pont registered trademark.

DOUBLE LIFE—
THE REEL WORLD

Twenty-one on Way to Disneyland Killed as Copter Crashes and Burns. (<u>N.Y. Times</u>, Aug. 15/68)

In his <u>Magic and Myth of the Movies</u> Parker Tyler explains how Mae West mimicked the female impersonator, heaping hellion upon ossification. Joyce devoted his eighth thunder, in <u>Finnegans Wake</u>, to the nature and human impact of the movies. His unifying theme is how Private Buckley shot the Russian general in the Crimean War.

The private eye of the camera taught the private guy how to shoot the whole cockeyed world. The generality of mankind can now be translated into the private dream world of anybody.

Ben Turpin, the cyclops, is the perfect image of the transforming and metamorphic power of the movies to create a vast harem for the King of Caractacus. (The mobility of the movies was surpassed by the car-act of the Twenties.)

"Such was the act of Goth." (<u>FW</u>)

Now you can afford to lead a double life.

Double Life Suits are now 85.

(Regularly $95)

The Browning Double Life Suit comes in pure wool cheviots, so you wear it as a regular business suit. But it also comes with extra flannel Slacks in solid shades that harmonize with the jacket, so you have a sports outfit, too. The suit fabric comes in every man's favorite weaves: including herringbones, windowpanes, glens, twills. The model is our natural shoulder Cambridge. Finally, we've reduced the regular $95 price of the Browning Double Life Suit to 85.00. Two outfits for less than the price of one. How can you resist leading a double life now?

Browning Fifth Avenue

How to be well dressed
without really
trying.

TO THE BLIND
ALL THINGS ARE SUDDEN

The constitution is all framed as visual culture as expounded by De Tocqueville. Practical politics are all tribal aural-oral as shown by M. Ostrogorski. Is it not like the clash between British and American libel law? In British common-law tradition (oral), "the greater the truth the greater the libel." In American written law, libel is split producer-consumer style: (a) was malice involved? (b) was harm sustained?

"Faith comes by hearing."

There never was a sceptic or an agnostic in a pre-literate society, so the post-literate society in which we now live is also much involved in religion and the inner trip. But for those who live without sight or sound the tactile involvement and faith are even greater.

Arthur C. Clark's <u>Profiles of the Future</u> says by 1990 man will turn turtle like the cyborg. He will carry his environment with him like B.O. or an astronaut his capsule.

In the age of the organ transplant the definition of "death" has become problematic.

Heralding
a new professional doctoral program for the ministry at the divinity school of the University of Chicago

The role of the Christian faith and of the Christian church is under radical question today. Ministry cannot be carried on in the same old way. Neither can education for ministry. Theological education must be re-thought and reformed to bring it into vital relationship with the new situation.

Not only are Christian faith and Christian church under radical question, they are also in the midst of a lively renewal. New forms for ministry are being found, old forms are being revitalized and reorganized. Either theological education will be an integral part of this renewal or it will be left behind, preparing men for a ministry that no longer exists.

It is not enough to tinker or maneuver with traditional forms of preparation for the ministry. A thorough-going re-working of the educational program for ministry is required. It must be as profound and as basic as the changes taking place in the ministry itself. Such a re-working will not reject everything from the past, it will build on the best of the traditional. But theological education must prove itself as able to reach out to the future as is the church itself in the midst of renewal. The Divinity School of the University of Chicago

is attempting to do this in its new professional doctoral program for ministry. This is not a re-working or a strengthening of the typical B.D. program, nor does it use the Ph. D. as a pattern.

It is an honest-to-goodness *professional doctoral* program that has a different point of departure and that is totally different dynamically from other programs for ministry.

It seeks students who are honestly questioning the possibility of ministry today. It allies itself with the search for renewal in the midst of cultural crisis. It represents a new attempt to find better forms through which to prepare men for the ministry. It is not the last word in theological education, it is only one of the first.

Jerald Brauer, dean

Two problems of faith in the contemporary world form the backdrop of a professional doctoral program for the ministry: (1) the ambiguity surrounding the form and substance of religious proclamation; (2) the problem of the adequacy of existing religious institutions to mediate faith in a complex society. The shift from a bachelor's program to a doctoral level reflects the intention to take these problems in full seriousness.

A bachelor's program presupposes a body of knowledge to be appropriated and viable institutions through which the professional can make that knowledge accessible to the culture. A doctoral program undertakes a radical inquiry into the content of the professional tradition and subjects the institutional media to an intense, theological inquiry. Thus, the ambiguity of the theoretical and practical aspects of professional ministry called forth radical inquiry - leading to a ministry of theological interpretation. To this extent, the doctor of ministry is not a new venture in theological orientation; the more sensitive schools have struggled for years to enrich and sharpen their bachelor's programs in order to develop theological inquiry in all phases of professional

ministry. The doctor of ministry extends the logic of this long struggle to the structure of the curriculum—acknowledging the depth of crisis in the religious tradition by realizing the doctoral character of such a fundamental inquiry.

Gibson Winter, staff

The Doctor of Ministry program offers the possibility of a major breakthrough in theological education. The contemporary world demands new approaches to ministry from the church if she is to be faithful to the gospel. A reshaping of the traditional curriculum in training for the ministry is long overdue. The Divinity School has now begun a process where faculty and students alike can participate in the building of a new curriculum. It will be widely watched and enthusiastically encouraged by all who are concerned about the church's mission in the years ahead.

R___rt Spike
National Co___ Churches

Those who developed the new professional program at Chicago came to learn that minor revisions, minor adaptations of an old program for ministerial studies no longer would serve. They began, then, by making an analysis of the problems and possibilities in the modern environment and by seeking to determine what in the tradition of church and university might best serve to help the school relate students as ministers to that environment. The result is a program which combines renewal and tradition, which affirms elements of the old and rather boldly experiments with the new.

The new professional program at Chicago grew out of questions like this: how can we best develop the resources of this university, this city, this divinity school to help prepare ministers for the church of today? As the program began to unfold we began to understand that 'this' university is a symbol of an expanding pluralistic culture; that 'this' city is a parable of an exploding secular culture; that 'this' divinity school stands at a representative juncture between church and culture. And that at this juncture, through this particular program, we might begin to make a major contribution toward meeting general problems which face those who would serve today.

Philip Hauser
Director, Population Research and Training Center, U of Chicago

The new professional doctoral program for the ministry is an imaginative, perceptive and realistic program designed to help bring the ministry, and indeed the church itself, into a more vital role in the contemporary world characterized by urbanism and metropolitanism as a way of life. The candidate who wins his D. Min. will have survived severe tests of himself, acquired a secure confidence in the Christian mission and a new level of competence with which to function in an increasingly secularized urban milieu.

THERE IS NO
RADIO FREE AMERICA

The literate bias of America was noted by
William Cobbett in 1795: "...They have all
been readers from their youth up...." The
extreme visual bias of the legal profession is
notorious, as in the declaration of Justice
Holmes: "The radio as it now operates among
us is not free. Nor is it entitled to the
protection of the First Amendment. It is not
engaged in the task of enlarging human
communication." The same divorce between
eye and ear (a main theme in <u>Finnegans
Wake</u> is this same Royal Divorce of eye and
ear). It appears in <u>The Use of Poetry and the
Use of Criticism</u>, 1933, by T. S. Eliot: "What
I call the 'auditory imagination' is the feeling,
for syllable and rhythm, penetrating far
below the conscious levels of thought and
feeling, invigorating every word, sinking to
the most primitive and forgotten, returning to
the origin and bringing something back,
seeking the beginning and the end. It works
through meanings, certainly, or not without
meanings in the ordinary sense, and fuses
the old and obliterated and the trite, the
current, and the new and surprising, the most
ancient and the most civilized mentality."

BECAUSE THERE IS NO RADIO FREE AMERICA:

"Ours is the only publication which lets the rest of
the world tell its story to the American people."

Malcolm Muir, Jr., Editor in Chief

You won't agree with everything you read in ATLAS. We don't. Each month we reprint *exactly* what the world press is saying. *Pravda, Le Figaro, Der Spiegel, The Times* of London, The Peking *People's Daily*—and 600 more. And each month more senators, Cabinet members, international business leaders, newspaper editors—each month more informed people subscribe to ATLAS. Since just last year circulation has more than quadrupled, from 30,000 to 125,000. We couldn't attract the people we do, if ATLAS wasn't saying something.

It is.

Consider just a few articles in one issue —the July issue. Hamburg's provocative daily *Die Zeit* offers Jean-Paul Sartre interviewing "Danny the Red" Cohn-Bendit, the leader of the Paris student uprising, on just how a tiny activist minority managed to swing it.

Prague's gutsy *Literarny Listy* prints, and ATLAS reprints for the first time in English, a review of and a moving excerpt from an explosive new novel by Alexandr Solzhenitsyn, whose famous "One Day in the Life of Ivan Denisovich" helped touch off the current cultural revolt in Eastern Europe.

Epoca of Milan explains why all the seas are now at the Kremlin's fingertips and its belief that Moscow hasn't sent its fleet to the Mediterranean "just to get a suntan."

From Tokyo's *Mainichi Daily News*, how the Japanese have put together the world's second largest steel company and some far-reaching implications.

Also in this one issue: "Exposed in the Turret," the most exciting book to come out of the Six-Day War; Hong Kong or Death, the "most diabolical organization in the Orient" at work.

Each month you'll find humor, business forecasts, cartoons, poetry, fiction (hitherto not translated), book reviews, scientific reports, editorials. Each month these are what 125,000 subscribers see in ATLAS. We publish ATLAS because there is no Radio Free America.

We can because this is America:

Use the ATLAS Hot Line: If you would rather order your ATLAS subscription by phone, just dial 800-243-0355 and ask for ATLAS. There is no charge to you. The number works 24 hours 7 days anywhere in the United States. (In Conn. call collect 853-3600)

14

Rear-View Mirror

My name is Jack, and I live in the back of the
Greta Garbo home for wayward boys and girls.

PASTIMES ARE
PAST TIMES. (FW)

The content or time clothing of any medium or culture is the preceding medium or culture. The content of Greco-Roman culture was the bardic and the gothic. It boomed again with the Romantics.

"Who in his heart doubts either that the facts of feminine clothiering are there all the time or that the feminine fiction, stranger than the facts, is there also at the same time, only a little to the rere? Or that one may be separated from the other? Or that both may then be contemplated simultaneously? Or that each may be taken up and considered in turn apart from the other." (Finnegans Wake, p. 109)

Time, October 22, 1968, pictured children in Japan watching an American Western. Bonanza land is the natural image in the rear-view mirror for the old folks of the TV generation, i.e., those over twenty-one. Vietnam is the Indian wars of the nineteenth century all over again. Our new Western frontier pushed all the way became the Orient.

Horizon (Summer, 1968) is devoted to rear-guard actions, including the nostalgic "goals" of Bucky Fuller and Lewis Mumford, the population explosion, which is in fact the information implosion, and finally: The Raising of Armies . . . for fighting distant border wars.

Those Who Can't Remember the Past Are Doomed to Repeat It.

E.g., Read The Last Great Cause by Sidney Weintraub. Its theme is the participation of literary folk in the Spanish civil war. Now the literate are causeless. About time they looked into what caused them.

168

On a clear day you can see a long, long time ago.

ENGLAND, 2 OR 3 WEEKS, $300. BY AUTO OR RAIL.

A little imagination in the right place is like magic. You supply the imagination, we'll supply almost everything else.

England, to do your imagining in. A drive-yourself car, with unlimited free mileage for two weeks or 1,000 free miles for three. A London hotel room the night you arrive, with breakfast next morning. Guesthouse accommodations for 12 or 19 nights.

Or you can see the Isles by rail, with no limit at all on how far you go.

Either way, we'll fly you gently to London and gently home again. Any Friday, Saturday, or Sunday, April through October. May all your days be clear ones.

BANANAS ARE
NOT CREATED EQUAL

"Historical orgins are less important than people generally think, the proof being that neither Eskimo nor Indian dialects have any kind of privileged position." (Federalism and the French Canadians, Pierre Trudeau)

Julien Benda fluttered the Twenties with his La Trahison des Clercs (The Great Betrayal) (1927 and 1946, Paris). Pierre Trudeau points to the new treason of the literati: "It is not the concept of nation that is retrograde; it is the idea that the nation must necessarily be sovereign."

Trudeau as a federalist is a man of the new corporation conglomerates, or family of utterly unlike entities.

Homogeneity, the old ideal of nation, is useless in the global village of gaps and interfaces.

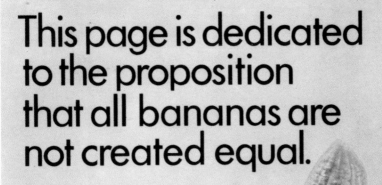

This page is dedicated to the proposition that all bananas are not created equal.

Chiquita® Brand Bananas.

A MEDIEVAL VIRGINIA WOOLF

Ride the World's Fastest Train Back to Ninth-Century Japan.

All in a Japanese Day.

"Flatchested fortyish, faintly flatulent and given to ratiocination by syncopation..." (FW)

The splendid Giacometti held by this modern Perseus is cast in the role of a snobbish addition to a worsted syndrome.

Away with the role of art as shield of vision in which to view and slay the gangrenous monster of Good Taste!

"To believe that it is necessary for or conducive to art, to 'improve' life, for instance—make architecture, dress, ornament, in better taste, is absurd."

The artist of the modern movement is a savage (in no sense an "advanced," perfected democratic, futuristic individual of Mr. Marinetti's limited imagination): this enormous, jangling, journalistic, fiery desert of modern life serves him as Nature did more technically primitive man." (Wyndham Lewis, Blast)

172

Act like you've always worn a Worsted-Tex®.

You'll get used to being a leader after a while.

It's easy. In a new gently tapered Worsted-Tex® traditional suit with its more natural waist to go with its natural shoulders. Worsted-Tex suits start at $75.00,* our lightweight Tropi-Tex suits from $65.00.* Worsted-Tex, 1290 Avenue of the Americas, N.Y. 10019

DON'T MISS AMERICA!

Miss America was killed by TV along with the Hollywood star system, and the political parties. Getting back to the first Miss America is like Leopold Bloom's idea for getting back to the Garden of Eden by knotting all the umbilical cords from now till then.

Volume 1 No. 1 of The <u>American Mercury</u> carried a now famous essay by Ernest Boyd entitled "Aesthete Model 1924." In the first radio age, art swaggered through the front door of a business civilization.

<u>Vogue</u>, June, 1967, asked: "Where is the Avant-Garde?" There was nothing like it.

Look Back in Anger: There aren't any good causes left.

Backward Christian Soldiers. (Malcolm Muggeridge)

Were You in Love with Carole Lombard? (Ad)

I need photos of every "Miss America" going back to...

(The first)

WIDE WORLD PHOTOS, INC.
50 Rockefeller Plaza
New York, N.Y. 10020

You'll find them all, from the first to the latest, in Wide World's collection of 50 million photos—50 million. Beauty queens and movie queens all the way back to the nickelodeon. Presidents and near presidents all the way back to Lincoln. Aircraft all the way back to the Wright Brothers. Astronauts all the way back to Alan Shepard. The catalog of categories goes on for pages, but you can have the one picture you need in no time. If Wide World doesn't have it, you'd be well advised to consider using a good illustrator.

OLD SPACE RANGER

When Pope Paul explains that the pill is a gimmick to make man a nineteenth-century machine, he is panned by those who can't bear the electric present.

The NASA space program, like Ayn Rand, is concerned with the old visual space of Newton and the eighteenth century. Purely retrograde and rear-view mirror. If top science is outdated, what about the print-oriented clergy?

The Ayn Rand cult has been noted as "quite the quietest and most hairless of all today's revolutionaries." That is, it is in visual "good taste."

The designation 'hairless' now fuses with The Naked Ape of Desmond Morris. Nothing could be less revolutionary than an ape, since at every turn it mimics something else. The Apes of God by Wyndham Lewis blasted the quite uncontemporary good-taste-apes who once controlled Bloomsbury.

The U.S. space program apes the old hardware economy of the pre-electric age. Electric space is not outer but inner. NASA could have created anti-gravitational transportation long ago except for the rear-view obsession of the scientific establishment.

Attention General Bonesteel, civilian coordinator of all U.S. military services and actions! The paraplegic paw of the scientific, military and business establishments is markedly present in this quote from Report from Iron Mountain: "The lack of fundamental organized social conflict inherent in space work, however, would rule it out as an adequate motivational substitute for war when applied to 'pure' science. But it could no doubt sustain the broad range of technological activity that a space budget of military dimensions would require."

176

A key factor in the NASA Apollo program, the Saturn S-IVB, operating as the second and final stage of the Saturn IB, will place the Apollo spacecraft into earth orbit. It will also operate as the third and final stage of the Saturn V, which NASA (National Aeronautics and Space Administration) has assigned to sending a manned Apollo to the moon late in this decade. S-IVB is 58 feet tall and 22 feet in diameter.

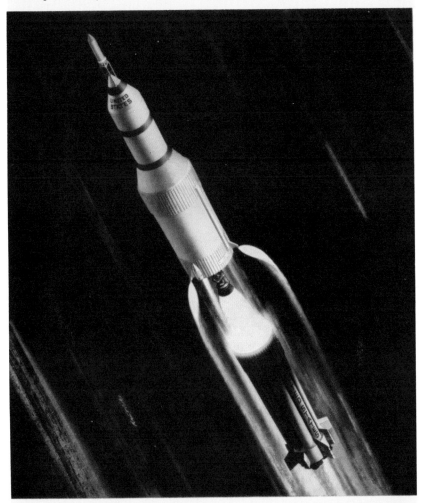

SATURN S-IVB is built by DOUGLAS

15.

Input
Is Not Experience

Who else but a Barth would dare create a hero
sired by a computer out of a virgin? (Blurb for
<u>Giles Goat-Boy</u>)

PICKING DAISIES

Like symbolic poetry, the present ad works by suggestion, not statement. It starts with the effect and lets the audience fill in the cause. Shirts are not featured. The implied shirts make you feel fresh as a daisy, etc. In the same way, the filling in of the gap between the old biological environment of our bodies and the new electric environment of our extended nervous system automatically evokes the world of ESP and LSD.

"Of necessity, therefore, anything in process of change is being changed by something else." (Thomas Aquinas)

When the evolutionary process shifts from biology to software technology the body becomes the old hardware environment. The human body is now a probe, a laboratory for experiments. In the middle of the nineteenth century Claude Bernard was the first medical man to conceive of le milieu intérieur. He saw the body, not as an outer object, but as an inner landscape, exactly as did the new painters and poets of the avant garde.

This is how your Forsyth Tacoma Permanent Press shirts will look and feel at the end of a long, hard day. Tacoma Permanent Press made by Forsyth. The finest in its field.

Forsyth

GOODNESS ONLY GNOSIS!
THE OSMIC COSMIC MAN

"...he was one of those lusty cocks for whom the audible-visible-gnosible-edible world existed." (FW)

Pushbotton Painkiller. Heart Nerves Wired for Transistor Slow Down for a Man Who Had Nothing to Lose (Life, May 24/68)

The Urb (Erb) it orbs. Smell is a total invisible environment. A happening. It is literally an electric circus. A perivallo, or striking from all sides.

Thanks Eversore Much.

Erb notes: "Our olfaction is tied to our past with unbreakable bonds." It sent Marcel Proust on an epic search for the osmic moment of the madeleine.

Martha Raye was more comical if she smelled geranium.

If you ever go to Africa, carry a spray gun filled with catnip. If, by chance, a lion comes toward you, it might help to spray him liberally. He could die laughing.

The victor belongs to the spoils.

by Russell C. Erb

*The
Common
Scents
of Smell*

**How the
nose knows
and what
it all shows!**

ALWAYS A COMPUTER
NEVER A BRIDE

Invention is the mother of necessity.

Beautiful Legs Instantly.
Computers Are Getting Into the Hair Care Business.
Randomized Love: "Two Hotels Adopt Computerized Dating."
(San Juan Star, April 5/68)

In his Mauberley (Life and Contacts), Pound presents the case of a man who never got in touch with the present: Unaffected by "The March of Events" he passed from men's memory in l'an trentiesmè de son âge.

Every language has a unique sensory mode of expressing plenary awareness:
The British: "I know it like the back of my hand." (visual)
The Russian: "I know it like the palm of my hand." (iconic)
The American: "...inside out." (kinetic, behaviorist)
The French: "au fond" (auditory, echo)
The German: "like the inside of my pocket" (tactile)
The Spaniard: "as if I'd given birth to it" (total involvement)
The Thailander: "like a snake swimming in water" (process)

184

Poor little Millie McIntyre is about to try feeding a computer.

It's enough to bring tears to a girl's eyes.

She might be a pretty young thing, a crackerjack clerk, and an asset to your office environment. But feeding a computer is not her strong suit.

But it would be, if you had Addressograph's automated data collection and input systems. (To put that in plain English, we make data recorders for 100% accurate input, and scanners to process input information at the lowest possible rejection rates.)

They're computer-compatible. But people-compatible, too. Which means clerical as well as non-clerical personnel can learn to operate them in a matter of minutes.

Our systems make Millie's work go faster. With less effort. And fewer errors than ever before.

So, to learn more, call your nearest Addressograph branch office (see the Yellow Pages). Or write Addressograph Multigraph Corporation, Department 6806, 1200 Babbitt Road, Cleveland, Ohio 44117.

Or are you the kind of a guy who can just sit there and watch a woman cry?

DÉJÀ VUE: FINN AGAIN

"Nature Abhors a Vacuum" (Ed. Hoover)

Bartlett's (long out of print) <u>Remembering</u> is a key document in approaching the work of I. A. Richards and the work of modern criticism. Both were Magdalene dons of yore. Bartlett tested his subjects by having them write down an inventory of any set of objects in front of them. They always distorted the scene. He had them repeat the same inventory at intervals of weeks and years, only to discover that the distorting process had continued in the interval. (Gap as metamorphosis interface.)

Perception or input is never the experience of "closure." No matter which sense receives the data the other senses rally to complement it.

The "New Criticism" not only discovered the sensorium as a laboratory but language itself as a shaper and distorter of ordinary experience.

New art is sensory violence on the frontiers of experience.

FUTURECASTER

. . . the key to the future is in this man's head . . .

MAURICE WOODRUFF PREDICTS!
SATURDAY NIGHTS 10:30 PM
WITH ROBERT Q. LEWIS
WNEW-TV

5

THE BRIDE SNIFFERS:
OSMOSIS PSYCHOSIS

"Do you Speak Replique?" (the perfume with a language all its own).

Many native societies rely on the services of skilled sniffers to arrange compatible marriages between the boys and the debs. Each human being creates a unique osmic environment that visual cultures suppress in the name of B.O. The appearances of men and women are not taken as seriously as their odors, in nonliterate cultures. Human compatibility and incompatibility, in any society, at any period of life, is mainly a matter of the silent language of smell. Olfactory space is a potent language that is never misunderstood. Olfactory space is a medium.

Metabolic change, in altering odor, can cause marriage breakups.

Edward T. Hall, in his Silent Language, discusses the smell factor in cultures, showing how it creates varied behavior. The Arabs, for example, consider it a hostile act for an interlocutor to be more than eight inches away.

The Archibald McKinnon experiments with natives in medical diagnosis (at Simon Fraser University, Vancouver, B.C.) has revealed their infallible and instant recognition of a disease and the organ affected, by smell alone.

U.S. military innovators have also taken to macroscopic sniffing for the human presence. "'People Sniffer' Follows Scent of Enemy from Copter in Delta." (N.Y. Times, Aug. 18/68)

188

TABU

the 'forbidden' fragrance

Dana

16.

Invisible Environment

Fish don't know water exists till beached.

A MESSAGE TO THE FISH

**I sent a message to the fish,
I told them "this is what I wish" (Through the
Looking-Glass)**

The hypnotic effect of yesterday's successes nourishes the bureaucratic egos.

A newspaper is a corporate symbolist poem, environmental and invisible, as poem.

Since in any situation 10 percent of the events cause 90 percent, we ignore the 10 percent and are stunned by the 90 percent. Without an anti-environment, all environments are invisible. The role of the artist is to create anti-environments as a means of perception and adjustment. Hamlet's sleuth technique for coping with the hidden environment around him was that of the artist: "As I perchance here-after shall think meet to put an antic disposition on"...
(I, v, 171-72)

Hugh Trevor-Roper explains the process of making environments invisible and invincible as follows: "Any society, as long as it is, or feels itself to be, a working society, tends to invest in itself: a military society tends to become more military, a bureaucratic society more bureaucratic...the dominant military or official or commercial classes cannot easily change their orientation...." (The Rise of Christian Europe, London, Thames and Hudson, 1965)

"Numbed to death by booze and tranquillizers" is an average strategy for "keeping in touch" with a runaway world.

192

Lockheed
is finding
newer ways to
handle the sea.

WITHOUT CENTERS OR MARGINS

The telegraph press mosaic is acoustic space as much as an electric circus.

One touch of Nature makes the whole world tin.

Auditory and tactile space have always been interleaved. If tactility is the space of the interval, the interval is the cause of closure and rhythm, or upbeat and downbeat.

Acoustic space is totally discontinuous, like touch. It is a sphere without centers or margins, as Professor Bott of the University of Toronto explained a generation ago.

Why was a visually oriented, literate, world indifferent to all but Euclidean space—until Lewis Carroll and Albert Einstein?

Audile-tactile space is the space of involvement. We "lose touch" without it. Visual space is the space of detachment and the public precautions we call "scientific method" and scholarly or citational erudition.

Jazz As Easy As Conversation. (N.Y. Times, Aug. 18/68)

Speech Scientist Wants to Use the Sound of the Human Voice to Help Protect Confidential Information.

Now—answers are friendlier

In fact, everyone in the company has a better outlook with the simple addition of Music by Muzak.®

Every quarter hour of Muzak programming changes by plan. Even your best employees get the lift they need, at the right time, to ease the monotony of daily routine.

Muzak requires no complicated on-premise equipment. No tapes. No records. Muzak programs come from one central distribution point. All you have to do is turn it on. And—your Muzak sound system can be used for paging and public address as well!

Unlike ordinary entertainment music, Muzak is a modern-management tool which improves communications, combats employee fatigue, boredom and tension. The proven way of improving on-time, on-the-job performance. Controlled tests have proved that Muzak programming can increase efficiency 8%, reduce errors over 17%. Write for details. *music by* **Muzak**

GIVE ME
THE MOON FOR A BLANKET

Soviets say moon soil can shelter men. (Toronto Globe and Mail, April 10/68)

A bedbug can detect the presence of a man two whole city blocks away, and a woman—well.... Our society is well known to the bedbug. (Erb, p. 51.)

"Happiness is for the Pigs" is the title of an essay by Herman Tennesen. (The Journal of Existentialism, Winter, 1966)

Anthony Jay quotes "Pussycat, pussycat, where have you been?" as insight into the tendency of people to reduce all reality to their own dimensions and interests. The cat didn't see the Queen, but saw a little mouse under the royal chair. Such is the clue in the headline: "Did Not Believe Nazis Killing Jews: The German Chancellor heard it all as Allied propaganda." (Kiesinger, Toronto Globe and Mail, July 5/68)

E. R. Leach, the anthropologist, notes that mere classification as "immoral" rendered 80,000 elegant London courtesans quite invisible to Dickens and his readers. They were a tourist attraction famous throughout Europe....

In the same way, both Stalin and Hitler were looked upon as saints by millions of their fellow countrymen, even in the midst of the holocaust...the Russian and German peoples simply "refused to know" what was going on right under their noses." (Runaway World?, Oxford Press, 1968)

Since Sputnik, the earth has been wrapped in a dome-like blanket or bubble. Nature ended. Art took over the ambidextrous universe. We continue to talk of a machine world.

196

It just sits there and does what it's told-

-230,922 miles away.

Surveyor, designed and built by Hughes

Surveyor, built for NASA and Jet Propulsion Laboratory, responds immediately to 256 different kinds of commands from earth.

HUGHES

HUGHES AIRCRAFT COMPANY

THE BOOK ARRIVES TOO LATE

The Concept of Dread, by Soren Kierkegaard, appeared in 1844, first year of the commercial telegraph (Baltimore to Washington). It mentions the telegraph as a reason for dread and nowness or existenz.

All the fuss and feathers about existentialism was the direct result of pulling out the connections between events as in a telegraph newspaper, pulling the story line of art as in symbolism.

The existentialist trauma had a physical basis in the first electric extension of our nervous system.

Professor Morse's telegraph is not only an era in the transmission of intelligence, but it has originated in the mind of an entirely new class of ideas, a new species of consciousness. Never before was anyone conscious that he knew with certainty what events were at that moment passing in a distant city—40, 100 or 500 miles off. For example, it is now precisely 11 o'clock. The telegraph announces as follows: 11 o'clock—Senator Walker is now replying to Mr. Butler upon the adoption of the two-thirds rule. It requires no small intellectual effort to realize that this is a fact that now is, and not one that has been. Baltimore is 40 miles from Washington. It is a most wonderful achievement in the arts. (From David Tanner's manuscript on Print Technology in America, to be published by McGraw-Hill)

198

The New York Review of Books has been called cliquish, intellectual, opinionated and snobbish. For $7.50 a year you can be, too.

For $7.50 a year, you too can be feared and envied.

What will your middle-brow friend say when you point out to him that his two favorite Book-of-the-Month Club authors, Toynbee and Snow, ". . . have one quality in common. They are more highly thought of by readers and by themselves than they are by their colleagues in the literary trade." (You need not credit A. J. P. Taylor for the observation.)

Imagine the reaction of your Jewish friends—any of your friends, for that matter—as you quote I. F. Stone's critique of Zionism in his article on Sartre's important symposium, "Le conflict israélo-arabe."

Or if you want to bring a Molotov cocktail to your next cocktail party, arm yourself with Tom Hayden's "The Occupation of Newark," in which the establishment ver-sion of what went on there is blown to bits by fact after carefully-aimed fact.

But controversial opinion isn't the only trouble you'll buy for your $7.50.

Could you admit to an ugly mob of Robert Lowell enthusiasts, his brand-new *Prometheus Bound* clutched, hard-covered, to their breasts, that you'd read the complete text last year in The New York Review?

Obviously, life as a New York Review reader isn't for everybody. Even some who become subscribers are going to be sorry.

To ease your regret if you should happen to be one of these, we've written an unusual offer into our coupon: a no-questions-asked refund of the entire annual subscription fee, that you can call for any time you feel like it during the life of the subscription.

Any time, that is, that you feel like thumbing your nose at us.

FREEDOM FROM THE PRESS

Are you brushing your teeth with secondhand water?

A good lie can travel half around the world before the truth can get out of bed. (Mark Twain)

Thanks eversore much, Point Carried! I can't say if it's the weight you strike me to the quick or that red mass I was looking at...Honours to you and may you be commended for our exhibitiveness! (FW)

British sociologist D. G. MacRae says the reason why the huge potential of the ad world has not been tapped by his colleagues is that "we do not want our prejudices disturbed by knowledge." If ads disappeared, so would most of our information service environment—the Muzak of the eye.

Like George Washington, Thomas Jefferson had a bad press. In 1807 he observed: "Nothing can now be believed which is seen in a newspaper. Truth itself becomes suspicious by being put in that polluted vehicle. I will add that the man who never looks at a newspaper is better informed than he who reads them...."

Death and taxes: Remember when you could be sure of them?

"Unless you've tried our embalming fluid, you haven't lived." (Ad in Casket and Sunnyside)

200

Creative advertising, creative journalism and creative readership, combined into one powerful selling force.

THE WALL STREET JOURNAL

Editions published: Eastern, Midwest, Pacific Coast and Southwest/Distributed everywhere every business day.

17.

Media Mix

Having adapted Beethoven's Sixth Symphony
for "Fantasia," Walt Disney commented: "Gee!
This'll make Beethoven."

THE FURLOINED EMPIRE

In his <u>History of the Fur Trade</u>, H. A. Innis explains how the North American colonies, British and American, were deeply indebted to the fur traders for their origins.

Washington and Jefferson were land surveyors eager to advance settlement of the fur traders' territories. Hence conflict. Settlers ruined trap lines. The igloo was also a fur-lined job. Until the trapper got the Eskimo on the trail, there were no igloos. The Eskimos still live in stone houses, ignored by cameramen as not photogenic. Multi-sensuous hunters, they proved the greatest mechanics at Gander, to the surprise of the American Air Force.

As the totem pole is tied to the lineality of the missionaries' Bible, so the igloo was made possible by the primus stove.

The Eskimo, like any pre-literate, leaps easily from the Paleolithic stone age to the electric age, by-passing the Neolithic specialism.

WHAT BECOMES A LEGEND MOST?

An exquisite extra-dark
natural mink called
BLACKGLAMA®
bred only by
Great Lakes Mink men
and designed by
Bonwit Teller.

"WE'RE SURE GOING
TO HAVE SOME WRECKS NOW!"

Disneyland is itself a wondrous media mix. Cartoons drove the photo back to myth and dream screen. E. S. Carpenter, in his review of The Disney Version (Richard Schickel, Simon and Schuster), points to another media mix in Disney's life: "The only splash of color in Disney's private life was a model train that circled his home....Much of his social life consisted of donning an engineer's cap....He enjoyed planning wrecks....'Boy, we're sure going to have some wrecks now!'"

The N.Y. Times of July 16/68, under the head "Steaming Along," shows "Rhodesia's Hot Prospect for the Olympic Marathon" training for the event by puffing along beside a full-size steam locomotive. As media mix this has all the pathos of The Loneliness of the Long Distance Runner.

The present ad mixes a dozen media but leaves us in doubt as to whether the commuter has slaughtered the plane pilot or the ticket agent.

After TWA Blue Chip Service, you arrive ready to do business in Chicago.

Aren't you a little tired of feeling like a commuter?

OXford 5-6000. Jets every hour on the half hour.

TELEVISION KILLS
TELEPHONY IN BROTHERS' BROIL (FW)

The present ad is more concerned with smothering than brothering and is as rich an example of media illiteracy as could be asked for.

"It's what's happening so don't fight it, baby!"

TV is not only an X-ray "zerothruster" or fire god like Zoroaster, but it is entirely subliminal in its impact, as is the case with all other new media.

The Reader's Digest portrays Prince Hamlet holding aloft a TV set on the platform of Elsinore as if he had encountered a spirit: Tv or not Tv? That's Not the Question. The reason it is not the question, of course, is that The Reader's Digest offers the advertiser a bigger market.

Medea Mystery: McLuhan's phone call from Roy Thompson (owner of the London Times) for a private chat about media. Chat blossoms (unbeknownst to McLuhan) into BBC show, also televised across U.S.A.

Some emotional arguments you hear about TV vs. magazines.

1. **Pictures in TV commercials move.** That's true. And there's a lot of excitement and drama in that. On the other hand, magazine pictures *stand still*. In case you have to sneeze. Or leave the room. And by the by, do you know who really invented the video-playback? Magazines did. We call it: Looking-At-The-Ad-A-Second-Time.

2. **TV is colorful and has impact for everybody.** Right. Magazine impact is limited to the audience you're trying to reach. Like, for example, women who want to read about products and ideas that help make them more efficient homemakers—and more attractive wives. They turn on Good Housekeeping Magazine for the precise purpose of doing just that. As to color: magazine color reaches 100% of the homes that own color-vision eyes.

3. **TV packs a lot into a minute.** It has to. At rates up to $1,000 per second.

4. **TV is the proven medium for new products.** What percentage of them, with TV as the dominant or only medium, survive the test market stage? We don't know. But in the past 4 years, 190 products have been introduced in test market editions of Good Housekeeping (all, of course, covered by our Consumers' Guaranty Seal); and of these, 73 have already gone regional or national.

5. **TV is easier to look at.** Agreed. With a magazine on your lap, you either concentrate or converse. *Not both.* You're involved. Or you aren't. And speaking of involvement, did you ever get involved with a magazine that reprinted last winter's entire issue as a "summer-replacement re-run"?

6. **With TV they can't turn the page and skip your ad.** No. But they can turn the dial. Or turn to human conversation. And besides, no advertising medium can make ineffective advertising effective. But the right environment in magazines can give effective advertising its maximum opportunity to be read, thought about, believed, and acted upon. Most important: when the audience goes out and plunks down 50¢ for that environment they're going to be doing some reading. Even if that magazine stays around the house awhile. And it does. As proven by voluminous research. And a gadget called: the magazine rack.

❋ ❋ ❋ ❋

Now that we've given vent to our emotions, let's agree that of course TV, when it's at its best, is a powerful medium that does stand alone in many areas of entertainment and impact. But in advertising it works best as part of a well-balanced media mix.

That's why so many advertisers depend on magazines *and* TV. Selective magazines such as Good Housekeeping. Each month, nearly 13,000,000 women seek out Good Housekeeping. They seek out the advertising. They believe it. They respond to it.

To advertising men who are also businessmen there is no emotional argument. No argument at all.

If you haven't already taken it, the next step is as clear as these words before your eyes.

Good Housekeeping

"IF IT WEREN'T FOR EDISON,
WE'D BE WATCHING TV BY CANDLELIGHT"

The invisibility of color TV, the supposition that it has some relation to black-and-white TV has proved a corker. Siegfried Giedion's phrase: "anonymous history" (in introducing Space-Time & Architecture) was an attempt to cope with the difficulty of introducing a new design form to people imbued with many unconscious habits of perception. Color is not so much a visual as a tactile medium (as Harley Parker and I explain in To the Vanishing Point: Space in Poetry and Painting).

The cones of the eye in interface create the experience of color: "The center or macula lutea of the eye is responsive to hue and texture. The periphery, on the other hand, is concerned with darkness and lightness and also with movement. . . .The macula and the periphery work in tandem. However, peripheral vision can exist by itself. While color vision is inclusive, black-and-white is partial. (The potential of any technology is always dissipated by its user's involvement in its predecessor.) The iconic thrust of color TV will be buried under mountains of old pictorial space."

On the back of this ad from TV Guide (June 8/68) Neil Hickey reports that "television is under attack for failing to communicate with the Negro;..."

Color TV, far more than black-and-white, gives the Negro easy dominance over the white man's image. Hickey is doing the usual. Ignoring the medium and watching the content.

A color TV set is only as good as the picture tube.

Most picture tubes look alike. And just as a pretty cabinet can enclose a poor set, so can a look-alike tube enclose a poor picture.

That's where Sylvania comes in. When we developed the original Color Bright 85® it was the brightest picture tube ever made. Richer reds, brighter blues, glowier greens.

And you still can't buy a better replacement tube. At any price.

So why take chances?

And just as tubes look alike, so do servicemen. But some don't always have what you need. And others are hard to find. The servicemen shown here install Color Bright 85. So when you have to replace the most important part of your set, don't let appearances fool you.

COLOR TELEVISION BY

SYLVANIA
A SUBSIDIARY OF
GENERAL TELEPHONE & ELECTRONICS

SHEEP IN WOLFE'S CLOTHING

Tramp covered with newspapers on park bench to buddy: "As a former media man, I use newspapers for coverage in depth and radio to find out what's going on." (Broadcasting, February 19/68)

At the beginning of his very flattering essay on myself in The Pump House Gang (Farrar, Straus & Giroux), Tom Wolfe has a drawing of me which at once suggests another title for his essay ("What if he's right?"), namely, "I'd Rather Be Wrong." At the end of his essay he confronts me with a waitress in a topless restaurant to whom I uttered the assurance: "The topless waitress is the thin edge of a trial balloon!" (I.e., the silicone bust.)

Anthropologist Leach is quite right in pointing out that the TV generation is "growing more conformist, not less." But it is not a visual or pictorial conformity that is developing. The hairless ape has begun to attach a great significance to his hair. "Fair tresses man's imperial race ensnare, And beauty draws us with a single hair." He points out that: "quite a lot of alarm is generated by sheep in wolves' clothing."

The young are really the hairs to a generation of incompetence.

212

HURRY UP, PLEASE, IT'S TIME!

"Assuary as there's a bonum in your ossthealogy!" (FW)

Time was perhaps the first magazine to apply the format of the telegraph press (i.e., the mosaic of items without connection) to the periodical. Just a dateline. The Time formula of mosaic in place of connected editorial features permits the juxtaposition of esoteric and trival — the formula for creating environments, not just a point of view.

Mosaic transparency and simultaneity appears in the ad itself. The mosaic as such is an acoustic, tribal form, feathers in the hat of Time.

"Only Time lets advertisers select three occupational cross-sections of its readers... (Note how the tribal caste system here bloometh.)

Only TIME offers this new kind of marketing selectivity: Demographic Editions

Only TIME lets advertisers select three occupational cross-sections of its readers and advertise just to them, with no wastage.

Like TIME's National Edition, all three Demographics go to the better-off, better-positioned Chiefs in their respective fields. Each Demographic Edition carries the same editorial and advertising contents as the National Edition except for additional pages of advertising addressed to the occupational group you want to reach.

As in the past, of course, if your primary market is Chiefs in every field...use TIME's National Edition.

Demographic Edition	Rate Base	Cost per B&W page
Doctors'	75,000	$1500
College Students'	250,000	$3125
Educators'	125,000	$1500

18.

Breaking Out
in Spots

If radio turned on the Negro in the Twenties,
TV has elevated him to imperial status in the
Sixties.

THE LEOPARD
CANNOT CHANGE HIS SPOTS?

Jack Gould, writing on television in The New York Times, March 17, 1968, headed his essay: Breaking Out in Spots. He was not concerned with the important news spots as well as entertainment spots that the Negro occupies since TV.

It is apparently unknown to the Negro as well that his TV image is enormously superior to that of the white person — especially on color TV. This is also true of the Oriental and of the American Indian.

It is simply due to the fact that the TV image is itself iconic. It favors the contour, the mask, the sculptured form. The play of light and shade in the white countenance, to say nothing of the habitual effort at individual facial expression, renders the white person hopelessly inferior on the TV medium.

As explained in Chapter 5 the tribal man cannot find an identity in a visual, legalistic culture. The Sicilian cannot create an image of identity in the U.S. save by violence. (The August 30, 1968, issue of Life is almost entirely devoted to misunderstanding this simple fact.)

Some American advertisers are color-blind.

Some advertisers see the Negro as a black man in white-face. What a mistake! The Negro doesn't respond to lily-white advertising in mass media. How could he? The Negro thinks black, feels black, and lives black simply because Jim Crow is still the national custom.

If you want to reach the heart of a $30-billion-a-year market, you'll have to recognize that the Negro is nobody's fair-haired boy. You'll have to change the color of your advertising. And you'll have to advertise in a publication of the Negro, by the Negro, and for the Negro.

That's Ebony—a magazine as different from mass media as black is from white.

Ebony.

The magazine that gets to the heart of the Negro market.

BLACK IS NOT A COLOR

As explained in the McLuhan <u>Dew Line</u> newsletter for July, 1968, <u>black is not a color</u>. White is all colors at once, but black is not in the spectrum. It is a gap. The Negro question is a red herring.

The spectrum gap that is black creates great involvement for all parties.

In a Wasp world of literate whites, black is merely a classification. In the new electric world of software, classifications disappear. The environment is fired at us point-blank.

The Negro has to scramble to form a new identity, as much as the businessman or the politician or the teen-ager. It is the quest for new identities (or the struggle to regain old ones — Bircher style) that creates violence.

This ad raises a multitude of structural questions. The mouth is the all-aggressive organ. Teeth are the most menacing of all human appointments because of their lineal order.

IS THIS ANY WAY TO SELL TOOTHPASTE TO A NEGRO?

Mention the Negro market to some advertisers and they'll tell you: "We're reaching them on television."

Exposing to them, yes. But *reaching* them?

How deeply do you think we can be reached by toothpaste that was presumably made for peaches-and-cream blondes?

How much can we care about any product that is always shown to us in a world we don't really live in?

How deeply can we be influenced by any medium that shows Negroes mainly when they are disturbing the peace?

Ebony reflects, for 2½ million urban Negro households, the world that Negroes really do live in.

It's not wholly a grim world, though God knows it has its problems. But it has its kicks, too—its pretty women, its successful men, its right guys and wrong guys, its vision of the good life. And that vision includes toothpaste and shampoo and food and furniture and cars and travel and practically all the things you'd like to sell us.

Advertise these products on television and we may see them. Advertise them in Ebony, and we'll *feel* them.

For the cost of only two or three nighttime network minutes, you can buy 12 color pages in Ebony.

You will reach 43% of the $32 billion Negro market — 2½ million urban households with average incomes of nearly $7,000 — a dozen times.

You will get continuity in a major market. And involvement instead of indifference. Is that worth two little minutes of your time?

If it is, we'd like to tell you Ebony's story with facts and numbers. You'll see why 80 of the 100 top U.S. advertisers include Ebony in their mass-marketing strategy.

It isn't because they're being broadminded.

For further information, please call: (New York) William P. Grayson, V.P., 1270 Avenue of the Americas, JUdson 6-2911. (Los Angeles) LeRoy Jeffries, V.P., 3600 Wilshire Boulevard, DUnkirk 1-5181. (Chicago) Lincoln Hudson, Ad Mgr., 1820 S. Michigan Ave., CAlument 5-1000.

EBONY is where
2½ million Negro families see their own life.

WELCOME TO THE MUDDLE CRASS

Negro Middle-class Revolution Subject of Negro-made TV Show. (<u>N.Y. Times</u>, April 26/68)

Jack Gould commented on the same show: "The changing mood of the Negro middle class from imitation of white middle-class values to greater emphasis on enduring black dignity and achievement was exhaustively detailed last night..."

Much later a panel of young Negro men and women reviewed the question of Negro home life as lived in the shadow of the American middle-class home. They stressed the fact that the uncertain position of the American father in the home created great difficulties in Negro domestic life.

TINY TIM is a patriarch compared to the suburban American Daddy.

Anthropologist Leach in <u>A Runaway World</u>? points to the basic fact that afflicts white and Negro alike: residential mobility. This isolates the household. "Family looks inwards upon itself;...there is an intensification of emotional stress between husband and wife, parents and children."

The loss of neighborhood plus the "matrifocal emphasis" makes a mockery of the advent of the tribal Negro into the consumer world of the middle class. He is detribalizing just when the white world is retribalizing.

We're dreaming of a black Christmas.

One of these days more advertisers will realize that the American Negro's blackness goes deeper than his skin; that the Negro finds white-oriented advertising colorless, unrealistic, unbelievable; that the Negro responds to advertising in which he can see himself — advertising that makes use of his hunger for status and recognition.

One of these days more advertisers will realize that our cities are growing darker every day; that Negroes already represent 28% of the aggregate central-city population in 78 key cities; that 95% of the country's 23 million Negroes live where 2/3 of all retail sales are made.

One of these days more advertisers will realize that the Negro is not the white man's burden; that he's earning $30 billion a year; that he spends a greater percentage of his income on food, home furnishings, and personal-care items than white people of comparable income do.

One of these days more advertisers will realize that Ebony discusses Civil Wrongs,

the Not-So-Great Society, Negro fraternal groups, Negro Weddings, and Negro employment; that Ebony's concern with the Negro way of life reaches 2,500,000 households every month, of which 34.1% of the male heads earn more than $10,000 a year; that 88% of Ebony readers never take home Ladies' Home Journal; that 79% never even glance at Look.

Maybe one of these days is Christmas. We can dream, can't we?

Ebony.
The magazine that gets to the heart of the Negro market.

*New York, William P. Grayson, V.P., 1270 Avenue of the Americas, JUdson 6-0911. Los Angeles, LeRoy Jeffries, V.P., 3600 Wilshire Blvd., Dunkirk 3-5181. Chicago, Lincoln Hudson, Adv. Mgr., 1820 South Michigan Ave., CAlumet 5-0900.

SLUM CLEARANCE AS VIOLENCE

It is only to the visually specialized man that there is disorder in a slum or in a junkyard. (On beautifying junkyards see Chapter 26.) The slum dweller, as any reader of Dickens is aware, leads a multi-sensuous life, even when there is an absence of consumer goods.

When he is transferred to a slum clearance project, he is as wretched as the convalescent in our bureaucratically organized hospitals.

The slum clearance project offers as dwellings tidy, hygienic boxes. Everything is visually organized. There is no neighborhood, even in potential. This major alteration of his sensory life destroys the slum dweller's sense of identity. He struggles violently to recover his identity. He makes a new slum as quickly as possible.

When the Black G.I. Comes Back from Vietnam is an essay by Saul Stern in the New York Times magazine section, March 24, 1968. War is education.

If the Negro could feel the equal of a white man when he is at the wheel of a truck, it is obvious that his ego is enormously enlarged when associated with a vast military team.

In the army, moreover, many Negroes have been officers in charge of white men. War is not only education but political revolution.

Johnny will never come marching home again.

224

Whatsamatta, don't you trust us?

For more than 25 years, Ebony has been getting to the heart of the Negro market: Business owners, managers, professionals, just people—people who buy razor blades.

To shave with.

Yet in Ebony's entire publishing history, we've never carried a page of advertising for a certain razor-blade manufacturer. White-oriented mass media has gotten all of the action.

That's a mistake. The Negro doesn't belong to a mass market. He's a separate. As separate as centuries of Southern hospitality and Northern justice can make him. He thinks black, feels black, lives black. No lily-white commercial has much to say to him.

Neither do all-white print ads. The Negro ignores the publications they run in, because these publications ignore the Negro. Sure, the "First Negro Ever To . . ." rates an article in the slicks. But the *average* Negro is neither recognized nor understood.

Ebony understands Negroes. The kind who sit on the Supreme Court as well as the kind who sit on the front steps.

Because Ebony gives the Negro what he hungers for—status and recognition and understanding and the truth—Ebony reaches 2,500,000 households every month: People who live where 2 out of 3 of all retail sales are made. People who spend more of their income on personal-care items than white people of comparable income do.

With this kind of an audience, it's hard to understand why our razor-blade prospect—who never passes up a chance to look sharp, feel sharp, and be sharp—has never tried to reach the Negro. Maybe he thinks the heart of a $30-billion-a-year market isn't worth talking to. Or maybe he's afraid that anything he advertises in Ebony will be used against him.

Ebony. The magazine that gets to the heart of the Negro market.

NEGRITUDE

She loved me for the dangers I had pass'd. (<u>Othello</u>)

"You read a poem about green grass, trees, snow, salt spray blowing up against a beach. Well, when we think of a beach we think of chicken bones, broken glass, beer cans."—Jerry Harris, an executive of the Afro-American Society at Rutgers University. (<u>N.Y. Times</u>, June 3/68)

Black is Beautiful. And It's So Beautiful to Be Black. It sounds a little bit like whistling in the dark, especially since the term Negritude sounds so very plaintive. In fact, this may be the flaw in "Negro," as if it were <u>Nego</u>— I deny.

This is also the paradox of the "blues" which serve to bridge all the cultures of the world. "Blue, accompanied by the shimmer of its complementary, acts upon the inner sensibility like the stroke of a gong." (Henri Matisse)

Since black is not a color but an interval, may this not be the ultimate secret of Negro mastery of rhythm? As explained in Chapter 9, "The Pool of Space," touch creates interval and evokes closure or rhythm.

In an article by Albert Goldman titled "Does He Teach Us the Meaning of 'Black Is Beautiful'?" (<u>N.Y. Times</u>, June 9/68), we are told how James Brown "has gotten so deep into the soul bag, dragging out the oldest Negro dances, the most basic gospel shouts, the funky, low-down rhythms of black history."

Most people prefer to go along for the ride on any trend whatever. A rudder needs to be anti-current.

BLACK IS BEAUTIFUL

AND ITS SO BEAUTIFUL TO BE BLACK

19.

The People Movers

The world is "cool" and home is "hot."

Motorist: "I'm never bothered by back-seat
          driving."
Friend: "What do you drive?"
Motorist: "A hearse."

"HURRY, CROSS THE RIVER
WHILE IT'S STILL HOT"

Air ad: This is the Time to Break Earthly Ties

Robert Turnbull's travel story in the <u>Toronto Globe and Mail</u>, June 1, 1968, was headed: <u>Striptease in Hamburg Something for the Broad-minded</u>. Contrapuntally beneath it was a headline from Alaska — <u>Porpoises Frolic among Icebergs</u>.

The aerial porpoises flip through much colder temperatures: From LaGuardia to Chicago— flights every hour on the hour and the half-hour.

Peter Kihss writes in <u>The New York Times</u>, August 1, 1968, under the head: Study Finds Nearly Half of N.Y.C. Families Moved in 5-Year Period.

Anthropologist Leach in <u>A Runaway World</u>? notes how in pre-railway days "most people spent their whole lives close to the place they were born....In the past, kinsfolk and neighbors gave the individual continuous moral support throughout his life. Today the domestic household is isolated; there is an intensification of emotional stress between husband and wife, and parents and children." At first, improved transportation broke up the home and then the neighborhood. The reverse of this in the TV age is a generation of children that feels completely at home any-where in the world—except in their own home.

230

The sun never sets on The People Movers.

The world knows Budd as People Movers—as a leading builder of railway cars and automotive components, and as a transportation innovator. When you get a reputation like that, there's world-wide demand for your talents.

Our big talent is production know-how. That's why manufacturers of 22 U.S. automobiles ask us to help build their cars. And we build rolling stock for major railroads and transit systems in this country. It's also why overseas manufacturers invite us to share our know-how with them.

You'll find The People Movers at work in the American, European, Asian, African, and Australian continents—serving the automotive and railway industries, and applying the skills we've picked up in such other specialties as plastics, paper, and exotic metallurgy.

What in the world can People Movers services do for you? Write or call, and we'll talk it over.

THE  COMPANY
PHILA., PA. 19132 • (215)—BA 5-9100 • Dept. 633

WE'LL BRING YOU BACK GORGEOUS

James A. Wechsler, writing in the <u>New York Post</u>, July 3, 1968, about a recent melancholy statistic encountered during two weeks of meditation on the disclosure by the Metropolitan Transit Authority, that the average citizen of this metropolis spends 480 hours each year riding the subways."

This Summer Half the World Is in San Antonio. You can ride in a Venetian gondola from the center of downtown San Antonio . . . If the glory isn't enough for you, we have a few things that are more practical. (Braniff ad)

Meanwhile, Technicolor photography enables you to feel you are there already: "Arrive now, go later."

Time Runs Out at JFK (William Burrows, <u>N.Y. Times</u>, July 29/68). Congestion in the air and on the ground threatens the future of New York's airports.

232

WE'LL BRING YOU BACK FROM LONDON GORGEOUS.

An English vacation.

You spend one-third of your time in the pubs. One-third in the museums. And one-third in the fog.

So naturally, you come home pale as the Canterbury Ghost.

Now, we're offering a happy ending to the English vacation.

A suntan.

On your way home from England we'll fly you to our home: Portugal. For just a few extra dollars.

There, awaiting your skin, is a sun warm enough to tan it in only a day or two.

And a coastline of deserted beaches.

Your travel agent, who likes to see you looking well, will make all the arrangements.

And, oh yes... we can also fly you from New York to Portugal. Then on to England.

In case you'd like to arrive in London gorgeous.

TAP Portuguese Airways

Americans, let us teach you how to fly.

THE CARSOPHAGUS

The Red Queen said, "...It takes all the running you can do to keep in the same place." You are one of those who just can't seem to get ahead of the game?

In an ambidextrous universe the person with a mere point of view enjoys one degree of vision. Once he breaks through the vanishing point, man moves into a 360-degree world of resonating Bucky domes. He can then renounce the buckboard bounce. Take the following example of how to slip through the vanishing point: Zena Cherry, in the <u>Toronto Globe and Mail</u> (Feb. 2/68), writes of two local families who have bought a couple of secondhand hearses and painted them brightly. "Up to a dozen kids and animals can play games and generally whoop it up in the back while my wife and I can enjoy silence and our own conversation in front of the sliding glass window."

Motorist: "I'm never bothered by back-seat driving."
Friend: "What do you drive?"
Motorist: "A hearse."

Our Paris or Rome packages are such a steal they even include a getaway car.

Take off into the country. Or wander the city. It's your car. You decide. And a hotel, for 15 nights; in Paris or Rome is included. Makes a great home base to operate from. Or call it a hide-out, if you prefer.

The jet fare, car and hotel is a 17-day package. For Paris, it's $320.* For Rome, $400.* It seems a steal because as an individual, you're getting the group rate. But Olympic Airways makes up the groups of 15 or more. You fly across and back with them. That's all. The rest of the time, you're on your own.

Your car (a Simca, Renault or Fiat) comes with the first 100 kilometers free. About 2¢ for each additional kilometer. However, if more than two occupy the car, you get unlimited free mileage. The Paris hotel is located in Montmartre. In Rome, it's near the Via Veneto. And there's show tickets, a free dinner, airport transfers and map/motoring information for each country.

If you want to make your getaway soon, contact your Travel Agent or Olympic Airways. Tell us which Saturday you'd like to depart. We'll need thirty days

to make up a group. Complete information on any of these can be gotten from your Travel Agent. Or mail the coupon.

*Based on 15-person group economy fare from New York. At certain dates, a higher fare will be applicable.

Olympic Airways Tour Department
P.O. Box 445, New York, N.Y. 10011

I've been thinking of getting away. Please send me the illustrated literature on your Getaway Package to
☐ Paris   ☐ Rome

Name _____

Address _____

City/State/Zip _____

OLYMPIC
A I R W A Y S

A SHIP IS A SHE,
BUT AN IRON HORSE...?

Remember the New York Telephone ad? "Let your fingers do the walking." In the computer age the role of the pedestrian is taken over by the pushbutton. For centuries man's work and his home were in the same place. His house consisted of a single room with beds in thick-walled alcoves.

Such domestic bliss has been by-passed by many subsequent techniques. According to an item in the <u>New York Post</u>, Feb. 23, 1968 —"Domestic Bliss Sidetracked By Home-Made Engine. Sunderland, England (Reuters) — Widow Janet Parkin, 66, has called off her wedding to miner Stan Kipling because he will not remove a traction engine from beside his bed. The home-made engine, crowned with the statue of a Greek goddess, is 62-year-old Stan's pride and joy — and he will not part with it. He said 'I want to work on the engine and add a few more ornaments to it.' Mrs. Parkin commented, 'I am being made to look a fool. I'm not taking second place to a traction engine.' The engine is about four feet high and six feet long."

Anthropologist Leach, whose models of ideal order are naturally tribal, greets the decay of the Western family with a cheer. (<u>Runaway World?</u>) Somnambulistically he is with the trend of the electrically regenerated kids of the West. (From six onward they could form little psychedelic communities.)

Live in Pasadena
Work on the Moon...

or Venus
or Mars
or Jupiter

And Surveyor VII has helped solve the commuting problems.

Right now, the men at Jet Propulsion Laboratory in Pasadena, California, are busy analyzing the Moon-data collected and sent back to Earth by Surveyor VII. Within minutes after its successful soft-landing on January 9, JPL's unmanned research spacecraft was shooting TV pictures under new lighting conditions and scooping up lunar soil from the most southerly landing site yet.

This mission was the last in the series of seven Surveyor flights and was probably the most difficult lunar surface probe ever made by the United States. Landing less than two kilometers from the target area near the crater Tycho in the rugged highlands, Surveyor VII was the first to investigate the Moon's "Deep South." Four of the previous successful Surveyors landed in the relatively smooth equatorial belt. They proved the lunar soil in that area is in many respects just like Earth soil and that it will support later astronaut landings. The most recent flight indicates that the southern soil should also support astronaut landings.

Admittedly, space experts don't know when men will actually go to the Moon. It's missions like Surveyor VII that land, dig, probe, photograph, analyze and accurately report the findings back to Earth which bring this date nearer. And it's men like those at JPL in Pasadena who work to solve outer space commuting problems! who bring flying to the Moon, Venus, Mars or anywhere else out there a lot closer. Send your resume, in confidence, to Mr. Wallace Peterson, Supervisor, Employment. He'll personally help solve your commuting problems.

JET PROPULSION LABORATORY

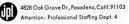 4828 Oak Grove Dr., Pasadena, Calif. 91103
Attention: Professional Staffing Dept. 4

20.

All Indians
Walk Single File

"Whats all the fuss? He only had the girl for a few weeks." (aristocratic comment in a George Meredith novel)

FIREWATER

African Nemesis: Right off Broadway.

Tribal societies cannot tolerate alcohol. The literate man needs stimulants to pull himself together, privately or socially. His visual culture fragments and isolates him. The tribal man is so integral, and so involved socially, that alcohol sends him berserk. Women are in somewhat the same position. Being more integral, they need no stimulants, except a man. This is the reason why the present ad is quite irrelevant to liquor. None of the people portrayed here has the slightest need for the outer trip of alcohol. Inner tripping, on the other hand, is the great escape hatch of all tribal societies past or present.

The modern world is acoustic and tribal because it lives in an all-at-once time and space. The need to escape from <u>Now</u> can only be through the looking glass into a timeless world of <u>déjà vu</u>, which is not unlike the stone age world of ads provided by Madison Avenue.

Anthropologist Marshall D. Sahlins has a dramatized spoof on: "Robert Ardrey: Former dramatist. Now leader of a revolutionary movement to reveal the true animal nature of man." (From <u>Man and Aggression</u>, edited by Ashley Montagu, Oxford University Press, 1968.)

NOW:

APOLOGIES TO THE IROQUOIS

Edmund Wilson's <u>Apologies to the Iroquois</u>, with a "Study of the Mohawks in High Steel" by Joseph Mitchell, stresses the new tribalism that animates the North American Indians: "The nationalist movement of the Iroquois is only one of many recent evidences of a new self-assertion on the part of the Indians."

Today there are nationalist movements in Quebec and Wales and Scotland and in every place that harbors tribal memories or acoustic resonance.

Radio and TV enormously increased the consciousness of the auditory space, and spurred an involvement that extended to the revival of ancient religions among several of the Indian nations of this continent. Creating their own space, they insist that they are not living in the United States or Canada.

What prompted Wilson's interest in the tribal resurgence was partly the efforts of government and corporations to seize Indian territories. It was also because of the strong Mohawk and Iroquois facility and nonchalance in working at great heights. (See my explanation of this phenomenon in Chapter 12.)

The new pattern of tribal conglomeration is the latest in the corporate business world, as well. <u>Banks Add Role As Marriage Brokers</u> (<u>N.Y. Times</u>, Aug. 21/68): "The mating of quite incongruous business enterprises has proved so lucrative as to attract banks into the institutionalizing of the courtship and marriage of business."

242

The American Indian

Indians, American, from Volume 15 of the Encyclopedia Americana.

TINY TIM

The unexamined life is not worth living. (Socrates)

Anthropologist Leach, in explaining the unbearable intensification of emotional stress in the isolated modern family, opens the door to understanding why in our electric, global environment the TV generation avoids jobs. It will plunge into any kind of menial or trivial activity as a way of joining the human-family-at-large, while avoiding any specialized support of the Establishment.

Tiny Tim has a name that expresses a world of grievance. His own act consists of singing like a pre-puberty choir boy and at the same time mocking the mellow voice of a suburban matriarch; i.e., the masculinized woman who has robbed him of his sex.

There is a considerable parallel with Mae West, the souped-up blonde who played the role of the female impersonator in order to mock the homosexuals and the world that made them.

British mores permit a playful sliding over the sexual scale from hetero- to homosexual that is not possible in "uptight" U.S. The British upper and lower classes have never been detribalized, and so "sex" is not a very serious matter with them.

The remark of Socrates cited above indicates the onset of visual cultural bias. Neither Socrates nor Plato was aware that analytic impulses, and the isolated examination of the private self, are the effect of phonetic literacy. So much for their own unexamined lives.

244

SCOTS WHA HAE

Stewart Alsop, in the <u>Saturday Evening Post</u> (July 27/68), tells of a "clan" that "is 300 years old and has produced presidents, poets and a privateer, monarchists, millionaires and a murderer."

Clans have corporate memories. They live "history as she is harped." There is for them no perspective, but just a great echo chamber of gossip and anecdote. Naturally, all members of a tribe are descended from kings. The head of a clan is a king constituted by the corporate participation of all the members of the clan. He has no private or legal existence. It is the same in the entertainment world and in the American Negro world, as Albert Goldman explains in <u>The New York Times</u> (June 9/68):

"Success in the Negro world, however, is always equated with royalty; so Brown makes a great show of his clothes (500 suits, 300 pairs of shoes), his cars (blue-black Mark III Continental, purple and silver-gray Rolls-Royce, Cadillac convertible, Eldorado, Toronado, Rambler), his twin-engine Lear jet, his two radio stations and his moated, drawbridged castle in St. Albans, Queens. Until recently, he regularly had himself crowned on stage and sat cheerfully on a throne, wearing ermine-trimmed robes."

That is the significance of Pilate's civilized Roman insistence on smacking at the tribal Israel by <u>writing</u>: "What I have written I have written." (John 19:22). Today the highly civilized and detribalized European Israeli are juxtaposed with intensely tribalized Arab clans. The gap or interface there creates the utmost stress and misunderstanding.

Princes Street in Edinburgh. Gordon Highlanders in foreground, Edinburgh Castle in the background.

Scotsmen are irresistible

Maybe it's because they can't resist *you*. They think American accents are quaint. And visitors give them a perfect opportunity to hold forth on their favorite topic —Scotland.

Ply Loch Lomond's waters on a four-hour steamer cruise (cost: $1.50); the Scotsman next to you at the railing may appoint himself your personal guide to the local legends.

Cheer out loud at the Highland Games (entrance fee, about 43¢); that Highlander at your side may welcome you into the clan. Or visit Ayrshire and drop in at one of Rabbie Burns' favorite taverns. Cost for a Scottish scotch and soda, 36¢.

Ask someone in Edinburgh the way to the Castle. He'll likely walk you there himself, to show off the view of the "new" 18th-century city from Castle Rock. He may also urge you to stroll the Royal Mile, hub of the "old" medieval city, to the Palace of Holyroodhouse—the Royal residence. He'll be as proud of these sites as if they all belonged to him. And they all do. Scotland is loyal to the British Queen, but it belongs to the Scots. They have their own legal system, their own banknotes —and, as you'll find, their own irresistible charm.

To learn more about Scotland, send for the free 52-page color guide, *Vacations in Britain*. And see your travel agent.

Please print and include zip code.

British Travel, Box 4100, New York, N.Y. 10017

TO: 506

NAME

ADDRESS

CITY   STATE   ZIP

LIFE IN THE
AMBIDEXTROSE UNIVERSE

"Blowing both horns of his dilemma."
(Harley Parker)

The copy of a Century cigarette ad under a somber tribal visage:
"Hi. I'm Ivan the Terrible. In the 1500's I became the first Czar of
Russia and I started war after war after war. How dull. Let me tell
you of a really exciting Century."

**The miniskirt, one of the more spectacular
tribal phenomena of our time, got tangled
with the Eucharistic Congress in Bogota,
Colombia: Miniskirted uniforms worn by
official hostesses at the 39th International
Eucharistic Congress raised eyebrows
yesterday among Roman Catholic dignitaries.
"A profanation," was the reaction of some of
the Cardinals and bishops....
The hostesses and uniforms were selected by
the Colombian Government, which is the
unofficial host to the Congress. The girls are
assigned to help visiting prelates find their
way around. (N.Y. Times, Aug. 21/68)**

Dulce et decorum est pro pontiff strippi!

**The present ad is a tear-jerker. Where are the
Humforfrees and Dumb-for-free of yesteryear?
How can he decide which face to put forward
when his script writers keep making him see
double? Is it possible to convert "NIX" into
"Yup" by mirrors? Or can it be done by barbed
wireless? Is the war winning?**

If we won World War I it was thanks to Charlie Chaplin. (B. Cendrars)

248

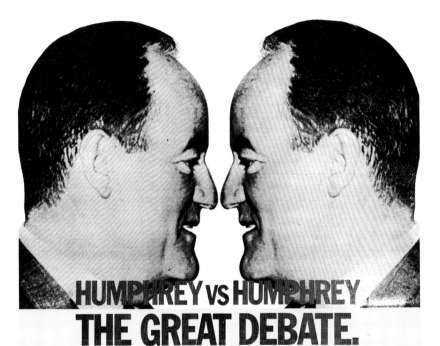

HUMPHREY vs HUMPHREY
THE GREAT DEBATE.

"What kind of world do you think it would be if the U.S. didn't stand guard around the world?"
as reported by N.E.T., Oct. 18, 1967:

"I must caution the American people, we don't want to get in the position of being the world's policeman..."
speaking on Face The Nation (CBS), June 30, 1968:

Humphrey said that if he had to live in a city ghetto with rats nibbling at his children's toes, "you'd have more trouble than you have had already, because I've got enough spark left in me to lead a mighty good revolt under those conditions."
as reported in the New York Times, July 19, 1966,

"Law and order is something that is desperately needed in the ghetto by the poor man."
Washington Metromedia (WTTG) June 30, 1968:

"I have my own views. I have my own conscience. I wear no man's collar."
quoted by AP, April 10, 1966:

"There's no Humphrey program, just the Johnson program, and there are no Humphrey people, just Johnson people, and I'm one of them."
quoted in Saturday Evening Post, April 10, 1965:

Which Humphrey do you want?

Humphrey the Hawk or Humphrey the Dove? Humphrey the Dreamer or Humphrey the Activist? Humphrey the Independent Thinker or Humphrey the Administration Boy?

What measure of 'andidate is this who plays double think on the gravest issues facing the world and the nation?

Deserving or not, such a man now is perilously close to getting the Democratic nod.

How can it happen when the people have time and again demonstrated at the primaries and in the polls their anguished disapproval over Administration policies—and their most ardent supporter?

Ask the delegates to the Convention. Ask the delegates you had no voice in choosing.

Better still, tell the delegates.

For your convenience call your local Democratic club and register your preference. (Or write to us, and we'll see that they get the mes-

sage.)

What we have to do is make the delegates understand that the usual political flimflam won't wash. We are not going to be unrepresented by them. We are going to be heard.

We're going to have a choice. We're going to have a Democratic candidate of commitment, of purpose, of integrity.

We're going to have our McCarthy —and the delegates are going to like it. They *always* like a winner.

Coalition for a Democratic Alternative
983 8th Avenue, New York, N.Y. 10019. Tel. 757-8715
I want to help.
Enclosed is my contribution of:
☐ $100 ☐ $50 ☐ $25 ☐ $10 ☐ $5
☐ Let me know where I can work for McCarthy in my community.
(Special skill or background.) _____
Name _____
Address _____
City _____ State _____ Zip _____
Make checks payable to:
"Coalition for A Democratic Alternative" or to "McCarthy for President"

Co-Executive Directors: Sarah Kovner, Harold Ickes.

21

The West Shall
Shake the East Awake

When you are riding an elephant, be sure not
to say... "The Amber Palace,
and step on it."

YES, WE HAVE NO NIRVANAS

"That Guru playing a sitar may be a New Yorker." "India Gives Culture, Gets $." "In Macy's at the Tiger Shop, a customer is fitted with a Nehru jacket, the 'in' look in the fashion industry now." "Air Pollution Cases in the First Half of '68 Top All '67's Total." (N.Y. Times, July 31/68)

Question: "What sort of barriers do you see to Westerners appreciating Indian music?"

Shankar: "Well, I find the barriers less and less nowadays, thanks to the young people." "I am very thankful to the Beatles..." "Now I can talk. But it was difficult at that time when I opened my mouth against the drugs and music together." (Eye magazine, May, 1968)

Music is <u>now</u> drug enough for anybody. Nature-boy music can run the full gamut from the whirling whine of a mosquito to the mechanical rigor of the cicada.

By comparison with China and Japan, the Indian culture is visual. They have eleven-hour movies. Their concept of the "self" as continuous with the cosmos is that of pictorial space. The integration of the "self" is achieved by obliteration.

India offers some reasonable flights from reality.

We'd like to take you out of your usual world. To bejeweled palaces. To temples whose carvings celebrate the totality of Life. To where rivers are goddesses and there's a rainbow worth of color around every marketplace.

And we've more than one way of taking you. Seven, in fact. Each different. And each includes your round-trip jet fare from New York.

Different in what facets of India you choose to see. How you'll get around. Where you stay. The time you want to take. And how much you'll spend. And that could be a lot less than you thought.

For a complete idea of how far from your reality we can take you, please mail the coupon for the brochure on the tour that interests you.

☐ 17 days. $838. Delhi, Agra, Sanchi, Ajanta, Ellora and Bombay. Departures from December, 1969 through April, 1970.

☐ 29 days. $725. Two itineraries available from November 1, 1969 through March, 1971. One takes you to the principal cities of North and Western India. The other covers Southern India.

☐ 29 days. $1569. Fully escorted tour of India, Russia, Nepal and Ceylon.

☐ 17 days. From $888. All inclusive tour of Bombay, Aurangabad, Udaipur, Jaipur, Agra, Delhi.

☐ 24-29 day fully escorted tour featuring the Art treasures of India and Nepal or Ceylon. Departures February 11, 1970 and March 11, 1970.

☐ 29 days. $1595. Fully escorted tour of India plus Iran and Nepal. Monthly departures from November, 1969 through October, 1971.

☐ 57 days. $4155. All inclusive, fully escorted tour of India, Nepal, Ceylon and Iran.

WEARING NO. 9
IN YANGTZE HATS

"Chinese Have Bigger Brains than Whites."
(<u>N.Y. Times</u>, June 30/68)

War Spurs Economics of a Struggling Asia. "...the turmoil in China stirred a flight of capital from Hong Kong for a time, but the Viet Nam war appears to be having a more profound effect on the economics of Asia." (<u>N.Y. Times</u>, Jan. 22/68)

Visitor Finds Hanoi a Sober City, Where Free Enterprise Coexists with Communism.
(William C. Baggs, <u>N.Y. Times</u>, April 12/68)

"...Even had Chiang Kai-shek exterminated his Chinese enemies with American help, it is probable that his basic anti-Western attitudes, vividly illustrated in these volumes, would have led eventually to dangerous conflict between the United States and China." (Brand Blanshard, <u>N.Y. Times</u>, Book Review, Feb. 25/68)

"Americans Bringing a Touch of Suburbia
to Laos." (<u>N.Y. Times</u>, May 17/68)

"American and Eastern Dances Commingled at Jacobs Pillow." Dan McDonagh, writing in <u>The New York Times</u>, July 31, 1968: "...I would suggest that it is a fruitless path of choreography to pursue."

"Japanese Growth Slows to a Gallop."
(Robert Trumbull, <u>N.Y. Times</u>, January 19/68)

254

DANSK STARTS A REVOLUTION IN CHINA

About time.

For the last few thousand years, China has been thought of as necessarily pale, frail and fragile. Delicate eggshell stuff that you could see a candle's light through. Refined. Overly refined.

So much for the past.

Today we appreciate objects for the natural quality of their materials. We see beauty in the grain of oiled teak, the unbroken curve of a steel or silver spoon, the accidental texture of handwoven linen.

Now, to match this mood, Dansk commissioned famed designer Niels Refsgaard to create *unaffected* China.

The material itself makes its own surprises. Those specks, for instance, are left by minerals that kiln-firing burned from the clay. The irregular surface that catches the play of light is the mark of hand-throwing, hand-glazing. No two pieces can ever be identical.

This is the China that goes with the life you lead, from Saturday night to Sunday morning. And on through the week. China that can glamorize a knockwurst or understate caviar.

We call it Generation, because we think it might start something. Most Dansk Designs do. It costs $18.95 for a five-piece place setting. Also comes in four patterns, slightly higher in cost. We make all the serving pieces you could want. (When you see them you'll want them all.)

To start your own tabletop revolution, send 10¢ for our new color catalog of 493 ideas. Write to Dansk Designs Ltd, Department YN, Mt. Kisco, N.Y. ● REG. TM DANSK DESIGNS LTD

UNSCREWING THE INSCRUTABLE EAST

"We see what is behind our eyes." (Chinese saying)

Denounce Student of Sherlock Holmes, "Watchdog of the British Bourgeoisie" (N.Y. Times). The Chinese antagonism to Holmes occurred when a Chinese official wanted his agents to study the methods of Sherlock. Today the "Red" Chinese have wrecked their cultural program of the past decade by failure to understand the psychic effects of their own written characters on mental processes and sensibility. They assumed that literacy was literacy in any language. Holmes could have saved them. His method was that of the artist: work backward from effect to the cause. The Chinese written character is tactile and iconic, not visual. Today the Japanese have taken over the oriental ascendancy and sensitivity.

Moriyama has been assigned the task at Toronto's super-zoo: "Tigers and deadly insects will make chilling eyeball-to-eyeball contact with humans ... most zoos tend to treat visitors like spectators." Moriyama: "A building should be like a strip-tease.... Nothing should be revealed at once." In one of his buildings "all the screw heads in the place ran East-West." In his Civic Garden Centre, "Everyone thought the thing was going to fall down....I wanted to get a natural, horticultural effect." (Betty Lee, Toronto Globe and Mail, July 13/68)

256

Starting now, East is West

Bates brings you the splendor of the East in this fabulous new "Lotus Blossom" bedspread. It *is* the Orient—lovely lotus pattern with puffy, hand-embroidered look...heavy welted border ...sunlit colors. Plus new improvements: Bates makes "Lotus Blossom" in extra length and generous width for today's modern beds. And you can machine-wash-and-dry the whole thing!

Bates

BARBECUE, CHOPSTICK STYLE

"After Hiroshima it was obvious that the loyalty of science was not to humanity but to truth—its own truth—and that the law of science was not the law of the good...but the law of the possible...what it is possible for technology to do technology will have done." (Archibald MacLeish, <u>Saturday Review</u>, July 23/68)

A Japanese child psychiatrist, noting the extreme rarity of reading disability among Japanese children, has suggested that the disability may be the result of the language used rather than of neurological disorder. (Jane E. Brody, <u>N.Y. Times</u>, July 23/68)

Western literacy specializes in the visual sense alone. Our children must learn to suppress their tactile and acoustic senses in order to acquire phonetic literacy. Dyslexia and near-point, etc., result. No studies of this kind have been made by Western psychologists. They assume the priority of sight as a fact of nature, and are unaware of the source of this assumption in our society.

The TV child cannot suppress tactility. He is a problem to our nineteenth-century educational establishment and to himself.

258

East meets West! The place: Tokyo's famous Chinzanso Restaurant, where you can barbecue right at your table — chopstick-style!

Japan.

Come with us across the Pacific and meet your neighbors in Japan. They're practically "next door" on Northwest. In fact . . . they're up to 8 hours closer.

We're the one airline that flies to Tokyo nonstop from Seattle. (We make the trip in less than half a day.)

So, we don't think of Japan as being "Far East" anymore.

Instead, we say, "It's Not-So-Far East on Northwest."

Come see for yourself. We'll have you there before you know it.

In the land of temples and teahouses, kimonos and mini-dresses, sake and scotch-on-the-rocks. Where business is booming, the Beatles are blaring, and everyone bows and says, "Domo."

Take your pick:

Tokyo or Osaka. We fly to both places. And from either one, it's just a short jaunt to Nagoya, Nara, Kobe — and colorful Kyoto.

We've got new low fares, too. Example: just $684* round-trip to Tokyo from Seattle. This makes our "Not-So-Far East" something else. Not-so-expensive!

Your neighbors in Japan are waiting. And so are we. So why not talk to your travel agent.

Because now you know. It's Not-So-Far East on Northwest.

*Plus tax

Northwest flies to Japan from more U.S. cities than any other airline. (9, in all.) 23 flights a week to choose from.

It's Not-So-Far East
on Northwest.

NORTHWEST ORIENT
THE FAN-JET AIRLINE

"STOP KICKING SAND IN MY FACE"

"An Eastern humming sphere of myself." (FW)

In Kuwait the daily income of 300,000 people is one billion dollars. Every fourth person is a millionaire. Twenty years ago Kuwait was a desert ghetto. Today its standard of living far surpasses the U.S.A.'s. It is done with barrels of oil. They have tribal communism, like the new electrified West. They never had a nineteenth or any earlier century. They were always tribal, Paleolithic. Never Neolithic. Never specialist or fragmented or visual. The chair as a fragmentation of human sensory life has never replaced the cushion or mat for them.

In the twelfth and thirteenth centuries the Crusaders brought back Moslem science to Europe, releasing the energies of the first Renaissance in the thirteenth century.

The Crimean War was decisive in moving Russia out of the oral and oriental orbit. (Franci Venturi, Roots of Revolution)

In 1915 the problem was how to get the U.S. into the war. Lowell Thomas went to the Western front, where he learned that the pictures he needed of medieval cavalry charges were to be had in the Middle East. He found T. E. Lawrence, an Irish nobody. Lawrence kicked lots of sand into our faces.

Stop kicking sand in my face.

The Arab doesn't like us.

He thinks the West has been pushing him around for a century. He even blames us for his recent humiliation at the hands of Israel.

The sad thing is—he's got a point.

In three issues, beginning this week, LIFE digs down to the roots of the present crisis in the Middle East. This first installment begins a hundred troubled years ago, with the digging of the Suez Canal and Britain's entry into Egypt.

LIFE untangles a tangled period of history. Western armies invade. Western rulers exploit and condescend. Tourists and missionaries and businessmen flock to the Arab lands and transform the Arab institutions. Big and little wars drench the Middle East in blood. World powers play chess with the Arab principalities.

And somehow, the Arab-in-the-street always ends up on the bottom.

Read this new series and you'll understand better the Arab's rage, his wounded pride, and his long frustration. Such understanding is one reason why 33 million people read LIFE week after week after week.

LIFE

22.

News That Stays News

"But Doctor, your diagnosis differs from all the others." "Yes, I know. But the autopsy will bear me out."

HELLO, MARSHALL MC LUHAN

World's last trump blown yesterday.
Foot-ball crowd sees Heaven's ope.
Thousands hear call to quick and dead.
Not End of World, says well-known Red.
(Headline History)

Three customers enter a steakhouse restaurant that is a front for espionage. They order steaks, well done, medium rare, and rare. When the waiter brings the steaks, he stoops to one customer and whispers: "The Medium is the Message."

"Do We Really Know What's Going On?"
This article in the TV Guide for March 9-15
is naturally rear-view mirror. The writer
mentions "64 percent of Americans now get
most of their news from television instead of
from newspapers or radio." The writer feels
the lack of literary description of "a day's
worth of world and local events in the fullness
of their detail and meaning." Instead, the
viewer gets a "skeletal version"; i.e., the
multi-sensuous involvement of Dali and
Picasso, instead of photographic detail and
detached viewpoint of the visual man.
A viewpoint is one degree of vision. When
visual viewpoint yields to any other sense
there comes 360-degree involvement.

If literate newsmen and military bureaucrats pulled out of Vietnam, we could communicate with the oriental, nonvisual culture easily. A point of view is meaningless in the electric age. Orientals and teen-agers do not have a point of view.

"Hello, Marshall McLuhan? We're Having Difficulty Communicating With North Vietnam . Is It Our Medium Or Our Message?"

IT SEEMS HISTORY IS TO BLAME

When a big power envelops a small power, as noted earlier, the small power at once appears archetypal and heroic. It also feels and acts that way. This has happened many, many times—as when Germany went into Belgium, or when Russia invaded Czechoslovakia, or when the U.S. took on Vietnam or the Negro. The <u>Pueblo</u> episode is the reverse pattern, with a small yokel group seizing the citadel of a vast power. The pattern now appears daily in our newly tribalized world when the kids take over large bureaucratic set-ups.

Intelligence Test on Culture of Negroes Is Devised (<u>N.Y. Times</u>, July 2/68). Mr. John Kifner presents a report on a new fiasco test based on visual matching of data: "T-Bone Walker got famous for playing what?" It is the "See Dick run" level of awareness. The great Bartlett in <u>Remembering</u> tells of testing the celebrated memory powers of an African native. He found his memory merely average. Bartlett used only visual, literate criteria. The acoustic Negro would have no opportunity to use his powers in that format.

Mother Brown
has survived
the Civil War, the
Spanish-American War,
World War I,
World War II,
the Korean War, and
the Vietnam War.

We hope
Mother Brown
lives long enough
to see peace.
But time
is running out.
Mother Brown
is 116 years old.

ZEBRA ASSOCIATES INC. ADVERTISING
1180 AVENUE OF THE AMERICAS
NEW YORK, N.Y. 10036

THE AWFUL TRUTH

I.e., the news that is not fit to print.

Too Much Good News Is Bad (<u>Newsweek</u>, April 29/68). The story under this headline concerns reversal effect in the stock market of a "boom." (Running before the wind in a sailboat makes possible a boom flip.) Since ads are all good news, it takes a lot of bad news to sell good news. News is an artifact where media are concerned. Any kind of good or bad news can be turned on or off at will for varying periods. Political candidates saturate public endurance very quickly today. From convention nomination to Election Day ensures attrition of any candidate's image. Since TV he must go into hiding and hush up.

The ad here is a mortician's notice of interment of a medium. Caveat emptor.

"Are the <u>New.York Times</u> Illiterate?" (Title of Leo Rosten raking of <u>Times</u>, <u>Look</u>, Feb. 20/68)

What shall we do with these men? For that a notable sign has been performed through them is manifest to all the inhabitants of Jerusalem, and we cannot deny it. But in order that it may spread no more among the people let us warn them to speak no more to any one in his name. (Acts 4:16-17)

DON'T LEAVE YOUR FRIENDS IN THE DARK

A gift subscription to Saturday Night will shine out like a good deed in a naughty world. What's more it will bring them the same wry comment, the same astringent reviews, the same balanced political assessments that you look forward to each month.

Just tear out the attached card, put their names on and send it to us forthwith. We will give them a royal welcome to The Saturday Night Clan.

POETRY IS NEWS
THAT STAYS NEWS

Poetry is the means of opening the doors of perception on areas of experience otherwise inaccessible. The press provides the individual with pap and packaged opinions. In its corporate design of invisible patterns, however the daily press also provides new dimensions that are only revealed in poetry. Byron's <u>Don Juan</u> is an early newspaper mock epic. Browning's <u>Ring and the Book</u> is explicitly a newspaper poem, as Ezra Pound acknowledged in his <u>Cantos</u>. <u>The Waste Land</u> is a newspaper epyllion, or little epic, using newspaper discontinuity and mosaic to include East and West, past and present in a single moment.

When Gerald Manley Hopkins bursts into colloquial phrase: Glory be to God for dappled things — For skies of couple-colour as a brinded cow; He suddenly brings the sinews of English into play by strong gestures and abrupt incongruities of imagery, such as any newspaper provides regularly and unintentionally.

270

What makes a newspaper great?

TWO-FOUR-SIX-EIGHT...
WHO DO WE APPRECIATE?
PETERSON...PETERSON...PETERSON!

Ted Peterson is probably the only sports reporter who ever had a football game halted in his honor while players and fans cheered his arrival on the scene. Such enthusiasm, usually reserved for ruling monarchs and presidents of banana republics, is typical of the regard this modest Minneapolis Star and Tribune staffer generates among sport fans everywhere in the Upper Midwest.

Peterson's beat is Upper Midwest high school sports—a specialty on which he has more first-hand information than anybody else alive. He has witnessed every Minnesota state basketball tournament since 1925. He is on first-name terms with every football coach and most of the players in Minnesota's 480-plus high schools. He knows the relative standings of virtually every one of the state's 600 amateur baseball teams. He is, in fact, "Mr. High School Sports" to a million or more fans in this sports-loving region.

In season Ted has watched as many as 12 baseball games in two days. He regularly travels 5000 miles a year covering football contests. In almost every village in his 3½ state area, junior athletes and their parents know him by sight. In Minnesota, his annual rating of the top 25 high school football teams determines the state champion and evokes more spirited discussion than the national All-America selections. Mail by the bagful is dumped on his desk recommending candidates for all-state football honors (he's received as many as 350 nominations for the same player in one day). College coaches the nation over follow Peterson's reports, often recruit players sight unseen on the strength of his newspaper stories. On one recent University of Minnesota football team, nine of the eleven starters were former Peterson picks for all-state team honors.

Sports-minded Upper Midwest parents, players, coaches and rooters religiously follow Ted's articles, customarily accept his judgments as final. Perhaps more than any other sports writer on the staff of these two newspapers, "Mr. High School Sports" helps to foster the spirit which makes the Minneapolis Star and Tribune true "home town papers" . . . best-read, best-liked, most-respected . . . among the people throughout America's big, busy Upper Midwest.

Copr., 1957, The Minneapolis Star and Tribune Co.

Minneapolis
Star *and* Tribune
EVENING   MORNING & SUNDAY

625,000 SUNDAY · 495,000 DAILY
JOHN COWLES, *President*

THE CHICKEN AND THE EGG

"The chicken was the egg's idea for getting more eggs." (Sam Butler)

Anonymous Call Sets Off Rumors of Nuclear Arms for Vietnam. (N.Y. Times, Feb. 12/68)

Bar Association Approves Rules to Restrict Release of Crime News to Press. (N.Y. Times, February 20/68)

"But Doctor, your diagnosis differs from all the others."
"Yes, I know. But the autopsy will bear me out."

Government-Media conflict. Hillier Krieghbaum in Saturday Review of Literature, July 13, 1968, mentions the arrival of the terms "managed news" and "credibility gap" during the Kennedy and Johnson regimes. By the time this kind of awareness is cliche, it no longer serves to direct attention to relevant matters.

News is now making, not matching. The news of the sponsor is, at least, as central to decision-making as the news of the press. Another gap has closed.

"We'll return to our commercials after this brief word from the program..."

Maybe the world's oldest television joke isn't a joke any more.

Are 30 program interruptions an hour on daytime television really funny?

Suppose you're a housewife who's mentally 'tuned-out' because the interruptions have become annoying?

And what if you're an advertiser, and one of those interruptions is your very persuasive, very expensive commercial?

How persuasive can your message be if it's preceded by another commercial, and immediately followed by two more?

And in light of the cost, how efficient?

In the last five years, daytime television rates have risen an estimated 82%. Production costs have soared, too. $40,000 to make one commercial isn't unusual.

Television can be a highly effective advertising medium. No one will deny that. But the overcrowding, the clutter, has reached the point where its effectiveness and efficiency must now be questioned.

You can't saturate a magazine.

For one thing, magazines can print as many pages as they want. And they can increase their editorial content, to maintain a good balance between editorial and advertising.

And magazine ads don't intrude. People can read them when they feel like it. Come back to them. Tear them out.

In fact, most people actually look forward to seeing ads in magazines.

Every month, for example, almost 13 million adult women look forward to seeing your advertising in Good Housekeeping. What's more, they're predisposed to believe it.

Our believability, combined with our rather impressive statistics, has caused a number of thoughtful businessmen to consider a better balanced media mix.

With Good Housekeeping as a prime ingredient.

We now return you to your morning newspaper.

Good Housekeeping

23.

I'll Never
Forget What's-His-Name

"How many Caesars and Pompeys by the mere
inspiration of their names have been rendered
worthy of them?" (Tristram Shandy)

CAN NIX-SON BECOME YES-SON?
MR. STAHMER AND MR. ERB

"There is something in names that we cannot help feeling." (Boswell)

"How many Caesars and Pompeys by the mere inspiration of their names have been rendered worthy of them?" (Tristram Shandy)

It was Mr. Erb writing on scents that put me onto Joseph Kane's Famous First Facts. Cain the first technologist!

Harold Stahmer has written Speak, That I May See Thee. Joyce never ceased to resonate with the sense of his name and wrote a massive drama about the "fun ferall at Finnegans Wake."

The Eskimo, or any other aural native, says: "How could I know 'stone' if I couldn't say it? How could I say it if there were no stone?"

The cavemen of Madison Avenue have begun to get sensitive to the ESP power of names to shape perception and to control energies. Remember the leaden "Edsel"? The literary idea of names as mere labels of classification killed the Edsel and many a politician. The names of characters create a world: Prufrock, Babbitt, W. C. Fields (i.e., the john, inside out), Chaplin (chaplain), the priest-artist scapegoat, the Ford—good for any kind of terrain and any pocket, etc.

276

Ron Rico. Wasn't he the WWI Flying Ace who was downed by a single kiss from Mata Hari?

Heavens no. Although Ronrico does travel in exciting circles.

But Ronrico's a rum. A very light rum to be sure. Perhaps the lightest, driest, smoothest tasting rum ever to take flight from Puerto Rico.

Take us up on it. We think you'll agree there's nothing like it this side of the wild blue yonder.

For a 30"x40" color poster of this ad send $1 to Personality Posters, Dept. E-8, 74 Fifth Ave., NYC 10011. Void where prohibited.

Ronrico. A rum to remember.

TIRED UNDERWEAR

How can magazine features compete with ads like these?

Nearby in the same magazine was a rollicking scene: This Man Has Something to Give You . . . A Rotten Cold!

Next door was a plug for <u>The Lure of the Limerick</u>:
The limerick's an art form complex
Whose contents run chiefly to sex,
It's famous for virgins and masculine urgin's
And vulgar erotic effects.

The limerick belongs with Pete Seeger in the oral-aural world of audience participation. The Tom-Swifties had a brief run, but were entirely oral in linking outrageous bouquets of sound: "I have very few flowers in my garden," he said lackadaisically!

The appeal of this ad is quite outdated. It belongs to the fastidious snoot world of the literate-visual culture that found B.O. offensive as such.

Tired underwear?

Check yours during Underwear Awareness Time.

Does your underwear sag? Is it old? Torn? Tired? If it is, put some life into it. Break loose with some Jockey® upderwear. It's the only underwear line with such variety in styles and colors.

Take the Life® Hip brief (1). Low waisted, hip hugging for today's trimmer fashions. No-chafe leg openings. In red, white, blue or black. $1.25.

Has your old T-shirt pulled a disappearing act in the wash? If so, get the Jockey Power-Knit® T-shirt (2). It keeps its size and shape. After all, it's made with more yarn. Same goes for the V-Neck style for a no-show neckline (3). Either one: $1.50.

On to the Life Super Brute shirt (4). Tapered body, longer sleeves and crew-

neck styling. In a variety of colors. Just $2.00.

Wear boxers? Okay. We've got the Life Slim Guy Racer (5). It has shorter legs and side vents. In tartan, paisley or solid colors, with piping trim. $1.50.

And how about the TKO® boxer (6)? The TKO features a wide cushion waist band and perfect proportioned seat. $1.50.

Want color in your life? Get the Life Cox'n shirt (7). It's a lively mock turtle neck that comes in about any color you want. And in white. Only $2.00.

But if you're like many men, you're wearing the Jockey Classic brief (8). The special support a man needs with comfort, for only.$1.25.

Or the Thorobred® Super brief (9). There's pure comfort with this mesh-pouched brief. Plus support. Only $1.75.

So check your underwear during "Underwear Awareness Time." Do your bit to help stamp out tired underwear. Get the styles and colors you want all wrapped up in the package with the Jockey boy.

IT'S A BAREFACED LIE

Says a Revlon ad: So deceptively see-through, people will think it's your own fresh flawless complexion.

Make-up is metaphor. It translates one face through another via transparency: "And so o'er that art which you say adds to Nature Is an art that nature makes." (Shakespeare)

Finnegans Wake owes much to a nineteenth-century play by Sir Charles Young, called Jim the Penman. Jim was a counterfeiter who was able to accommodate himself to all levels of society by his forgeries. Joyce saw the artist as a forger who moved through all levels of experience. He branded his own Ulysses as "an epical forged cheque on the public for his own private profit." To this end he, the artist, had practiced "how cutely to copy all their various styles of signature." His artist is Shem the Penman: "Shem was sham and a low sham." The sham and the shaman blend artist and priest "putting truth and untruth together." It is by indirections that the artist finds directions out, overcoming the fruits of the fall that had put a "kink in our arts over sense." (FW)

The blushing generation wears

'Blush-On'

the first and only (can't-be-copied)
totally transparent blusher

Nothing turns on that 'real thing' glow like 'Blush-On'. The
sheerest breath of color you fluff on all over your face. Other
blushers are obvious put-ons. Only 'Blush-On' looks sincere.
Because the color is transparent. Like the real thing. It's made
a whole generation of beauties blush. As if they meant it.

'Blush-On' invented by Revlon

THE TREE THAT GROWS
IN BROOKLYN IS A FRAUD

To Brooklyn with Love

"Tell me tale of stem or stone" (FW)

This is the jujitsu style in advertising. Throw them with the truth. The copy in the ad concludes: "One final note: That tree that grows in Brooklyn is a fraud. It's not a native at all. Comes from the Orient. Just moved to Brooklyn and likes it." Earlier the copy had dwelt on the cultural and historical riches of Brooklyn, first settled in 1636, the year of the founding of Harvard. True, the two institutions have diverged.

Brooklyn was bought from the Mohawks, who later returned to put up the skyscrapers.

The exotic sounds of "boid" and "choich" and "shoit" and related idioms are old English dialect words, which with many others are as common in the Carolinas and New Orleans.

The tree that grows in Brooklyn is a fraud.

Brooklyn was first settled in 1636 by two farmers who got sick and tired of the crowds in Manhattan. They bought the land from a band of Mohawk Indians. There is still a band of Mohawk Indians in Brooklyn but they come from Canada.

It is estimated that one out of every 65 people in the U.S. was born in Brooklyn. That's why you can always get applause by mentioning the name to an audience. It's the fourth most populous community in the U.S. Indeed, it has more people than 26 states.

Brooklyn's 78.5 square miles take in all of Kings County, but the phrase, "King's English" does not refer to the picturesque local dialect.

In 1965 Dun and Bradstreet ranked Kings County fourth among the top industrial counties of the country, with more than 7,500 manufacturers producing well over $5 billion worth of goods. This is not counting the income of standup comedians who mention Brooklyn.

Brooklyn's harbor is one of the finest in the world. Robert Fulton launched the first steamboat there, and it is likely that a native gave it the name "Fulton's Folly." Today, some 5,000 steamboats visit Brooklyn every year.

If you hadn't thought about Brooklyn as a cultural center, you should learn. It has its own symphony orchestra and ballet company, three fine museums and a vast independent library system. More than 65,000 students attend thirteen public and private colleges, universities and specialized schools. Walt Whitman wrote and published "Leaves of Grass" while living in Brooklyn.

For the gourmet Brooklyn is a challenge. It is the home of the knish, the foot-long hot dog and the kosher pizza. One can find reindeer steak in Bay Ridge and blowfish tails in Sheepshead Bay. One had better keep bicarbonate handy.

Let's see now. We should also mention the 6,000 acres of park, the New York Aquarium and the world's biggest and gaudiest amusement center, Coney Island. Then there's the zoo and the botanic garden.

One final note. That tree that grows in Brooklyn is a fraud. It's not a native at all. Comes from the Orient. Just moved to Brooklyn and likes it.

New York is New York. Is there anywhere else?

THE ECONOMIC DEVELOPMENT COUNCIL OF NEW YORK CITY.

A DIMPLE OF DRY RAIN

If the only medium for poetry were granite, the effect on diction and syntax would be considerable. <u>Le mot juste</u> (the most juice) would be inevitable. The copywriter who has to create a new public with four or five words as limit may toil for months over a phrase.

Joyce's discovery that two clichés in interface release a flood of archetypes is often used in journalism, as "For Whom the Belles Toil" or "Generation of Gripers" and "The Wrath of Grapes."

Business has been hesitant to test this principle, but one corporation has publicly asked: "Look what happens when we rub the sciences together!" Naturally, the result is an art unknown to science or industry.

Verbi-voco-visual conglomerates now begin to appeal to the fun-animal world of the decision-makers. They must live simultaneously in many dimensions. Their entire attitude to language has changed faster than that of the journalist.

24

Slang

"In this bra you just suddenly have pizzazz!...
It's like whipped chiffon."

IT'S A GAS!
FREAKING OUT IN LOS ANGELES

**"The funny man is a man with a grievance."
(Steve Allen)**

Slang is verbal violence on new psychic frontiers. It is a quest for identity.

"Like I mean, you know," says the Human Moon, "these kids are where it's at today, man, and they know it, and I know it, and like I'm with them, and if they love me, it's only because I love them, and like they know it, and I know it, and we're in this thing together, and I'm with them all the way." (Tom Wolfe, in New York magazine, August 26/68.)

Like the artist-priest Stephen Dedalus, the clown is a probe. Whether it's Al Capp or Walt Kelly or Pat Paulsen, or the medieval jester, the clown attacks power. He tests the tolerances for us all. He tells us where the new boundaries are on the changing frontiers of the Establishment. The clown is merciless, without conscience, yet he gets our sympathy because he is a scapegoat. He uses the language of gesture, as in Tom's mocking of the hippie-hippo lingo above.

The whole TV generation is moving into the clown-scapegoat role. They have a grievance. They have been robbed of their old image. Slang is the verbal manifestation of grievance. Slang is an exploration of the new technical and sensory environment that is shifting the speech patterns of the old environment. Slang helps to shape the new identity.

It's a diesel   ...it's a gas.

There is nothing prettier than a Mercedes-Benz.

Unless it's two of them.

Consider the beauties above.

Identical except for the wonderful power plants under the bonnets.

At left, the 190 D. The "D" stands for diesel and for extra distance.

At right, the similarly elegant 190, with gasoline engine.

Now, if you drive 20,000 to 30,000 miles per year the 190 D may be for you. Here's real class with smart, business-like economy.

Proved, too. One of the country's top petroleum marketers recently put this car through a 7,000 mile fuel consumption test in a big city.

The 190 D traveled up to 39 miles per gallon in regular city traffic and up to 43.9 miles per gallon over the big city expressways!

And remember—diesel fuel, available practically everywhere, costs about 40% less than gasoline.

But if the idea of a diesel is a little too advanced to digest right now, you might think of the 190.

Here is the same classic beauty. The same quiet, enduring design. Simply runs on gasoline (22 m.p.g., too). That's the difference.

Automatic transmission, if you want, both models.

A LITTLE OOMPH
WITHOUT A LOT OF YUK

Where else but on the changing frontiers of the human figure should verbal experiment occur? Sloughing off yesterday has to be done by gesture, by pilot experiment, in science, in business, in education or in politics: "In this bra you just suddenly have pizzazz! It's like whipped chiffon."

Slang is the feedforward that tells us where the new frontiers of energy are shaping up. It is anonymous unanimous. No child ever made an incorrect use of slang. It's oral. Incorrect speech, "just between you and I," is an attempt to translate the oral into visual form. It is comic. Mort Sahl discovered that the reverse is also comic. Just read aloud to an audience <u>anything</u> from a newspaper and people roll in the aisle.

For the young woman who wants a little oomph without a lot of yuk.

LIGHT 'N LOVELY. Shapes you young and round. With Kodel. It's like whipped chiffon. Oomphie! In this bra, you just suddenly have pizazz! All because of that light, white, lively Kodel. It's like whipped chiffon. And, by the way, it keeps its shape wash after wash. Forget bunching and shredding. Yuk! That just can't happen with Kodel. And you know something else? Light 'n Lovely acts for all the world like a $6 bra, but it costs only $4.50 Oomph anyone?

Lightly lined Style
P4448 A32-36, B and C 32-38 **$4.50**
Also Lace Bandeau Style
P448 A32-36, B and C 32-38 **$4.**
and Fully Padded Style
3448 A32-36, B32-36 **$5.**

It's another live-a-little bra.

Exquisite form

QUOTH THE RAVEN:
I'VE BEEN ROOKED

"The hand that rocked the cradle has kicked the bucket."

This effort by an oriental to use a bit of slang is just casting perils before swains.

Many people listening to the World Serious (as the World Series is pronounced by some baseball commentators) have got the idea that the last two words of the National anthem are "Play Ball!"

The present ad uses a mass of useless verbiage just as TV commercials use radio-like intensity of sound that destroys their effect. The squawk of the raven is simply about a new chemical discovery that puts all cables underground. It ain't for the boids.

We anticipate some squawks about our new sodium cable.

But we're glad to lend the utilities a hand in getting their electrical systems underground.

What we've done is invent a new kind of cable. We call it Nacon cable.

It's made from sodium, the cheapest metal there is. Sodium's a light, excellent conductor. The only problem: it's reactive in water.

But we've found a way to enclose it in an extruded polyethylene tube. This plastic protects the sodium from moisture. And provides the insulation.

Result: a flexible, less expensive cable.

It's something we could do because we're so involved in both metals and plastics. And it's something that's helping make it feasible to put more and more electrical systems underground—so there's less and less clutter on the landscape.

Nacon cable is a discovery that ought to make everyone happy. Except the birds.

UNION CARBIDE

THE DISCOVERY COMPANY

DO YOU USE JUST "GLOP"?

It isn't so easy to get "glop" out of English. The bureaucratic prose of protocols and public legal precautions that pervades every business is an effort to plug the loogle leapholes.

Ads are plugs, but not for leapholes. On the page next to this ad was: That Eternal Ticking Can Drive Your Watch Cuckoo. We've Left Out Everything That Makes a Watch Tick. We've Replaced the Whole Works with a Tuning Fork That Works.

Next ad was: Is "slow" gin sloe gin? No.

Politicians use glop. It just sits there. It creates a link between their pillows and your hair. That is their way to feather a nest.

Do you use just "glop"? Or have you discovered Paradox?

Today "glop" is out. Definitely. Forever and ever. And why not? Heavy creams have a habit of just sitting there on your skin. (And besides, they're messy next to your pillow or near your hair.)

First sight...first touch...and you know Paradox is different. For instance, Crème Paradox. So light it floats down into your skin...is instantly absorbed. And blissfully, it works its wonders all through your sleeping hours.

Crème Paradox, Paradox Crème Cleanser, Paradox Skin Freshener and Paradox Moisturizing Lotion...together they pamper and protect your skin every moment...create for your complexion a whole new wonderful world of complete beauty care. It's the Paradox Principle of Skin Care... and, miraculously, it takes a mere six minutes a day.

Why not discover Paradox today? We promise: you'll be glad you did.

Paradox preparations are hypo-allergenic. Available at fine drug and department stores everywhere.

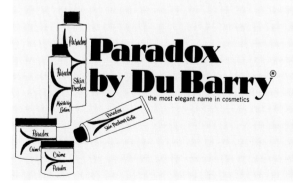

Paradox by Du Barry®
the most elegant name in cosmetics

THAT SHAKE-SPEE-HEAR-EYE-IN RAG

An <u>in</u> guy is one who has been prepositioned.

The random stone is that massive unmovable support of a printing press. It is literally the pre-position of the press. How did it ever get associated with the helter-skelter idea of random choice?

Remember ragtime? It seemed that all order and continuity had abandoned music in the 1920's: OOOO that Shakespeherian Rag— It's so elegant So intelligent....

In these words from <u>The Waste Land</u> Eliot uses the slang of his day to reveal the collapse of psyche and society. The great master of English whose plays had shouldered the Globe Theater ("spherian") had come to be banal. A bore.

Incongruously, shirt makers are here throwing the book as a new form of clothing. First paper dresses, and then ink spot globs of English as your label.

Richard Goldstein in <u>Life</u> (June 28, 1968) goes out for "wiggy wiggy words that Feed your Mind."

The New Rock for my bay-bee in the treetop.

THE RANDOM HOUSE SWEAT SHIRT OF THE ENGLISH LANGUAGE.

Eagle Shirtmakers bring you one well-defined word on one well-made Eagle sweat shirt, $4. That is all it takes to cover the real you with meaning. Define yourself. Your friends. Your world. There are 18 different sweat shirts to choose from, as listed below. Available in small, medium, large and extra large wherever meaningful sweat shirts are sold.

anti-, a learned borrowing from Greek meaning "against," "opposite of," used in the formation of compound words (*anticline*); used freely in combination with elements of any origin (*antibody; antifreeze; antiknock*). Also, *before a vowel*, **ant-.** [ME < L < Gk, comb. form of *anti*; akin to Skt *anti*, L *ante*, E *an-* in *answer*. Cf. ANTE-]

drop-out (drop′out′), *n.* **1.** an act or instance of dropping out. **2.** a student who withdraws before completing a course of instruction. **3.** a person who withdraws from high school after having reached the legal age to do so. **4.** *Rugby.* a drop kick made by a defending team from within its own 25-yard line as a result of a touchdown or of the ball's having touched or gone outside of a touch-in-goal line or the dead-ball line. **5.** Also called **facsimile, highlight halftone.** a halftone negative or plate in which dots have been eliminated from highlights by continued etching, burning in, opaquing, or the like. Also, **drop′-out′.** [n. use of v. phrase *drop out*]

ec·cen·tric (ik sen′trik, ek-), *adj.* **1.** deviating from the recognized or customary character, practice, etc.; irregular; erratic; peculiar; odd: *eccentric conduct; an eccentric person.* **2.** *Geom.* not having the same center; not concentric: used esp. of two circles or spheres at least one of which contains the centers of both. **3.** not situated in the center, as an axis. **4.** *Mach.* having the axis or support away from the center, as a wheel. **5.** *Astron.* deviating from a circular form, as an elliptic orbit. —*n.* **6.** a person who has an unusual, peculiar, or odd personality, set of beliefs, or behavior pattern. **7.** something that is unusual, peculiar, or odd. **8.** *Mach.* a device for converting circular motion into reciprocating rectilinear motion, consisting of a disk fixed somewhat out of center to a revolving shaft, and working freely in a surrounding collar (**eccen′tric strap′**), to which a rod (**eccen′tric rod′**) is attached. Also, *esp. Brit.*, **excentric.** [< LL *eccentric(us)* < Gk *ékkentr(os)* out of center (see EC-, CENTER) + L *-icus* -IC] —**ec·cen′tri·cal,** *adj.* —**ec·cen′tri·cal·ly,** *adv.*
—**Ant. 1.** normal, ordinary.

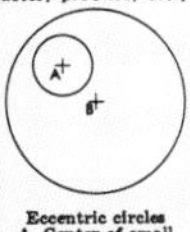

Eccentric circles
A, Center of small circle; B, Center of large circle

flow·er (flou′ər), *n.* **1.** the blossom of a plant. **2.** *Bot.* **a.** that part of a seed plant comprising the reproductive organs and their envelopes if any, esp. when such envelopes are more or less conspicuous in form and color. **b.** an analogous reproductive structure in other plants, as the mosses. **3.** a plant considered with reference to its blossom or cultivated for its floral beauty. **4.** state of efflorescence or bloom: *Peonies were in flower.* **5.** an ornament representing a flower. **6.** Also called **fleuron, floret.** *Print.* an ornamental piece of type, esp. a stylized floral design, often used in a line to decorate chapter headings, page borders, bindings, etc. **7.** any ornament or adornment. **8.** See **figure of speech. 9.** the finest or most flourishing state or period, as of life or beauty: *Poetic drama was in flower in Elizabethan England.* **10.** the best or finest member or part of a number, body, or whole: *the flower of American youth.* **11.** the finest or choicest product or example. **12. flowers,** (construed as sing.) *Chem.* a substance in the form of a fine powder, esp. as obtained by sublimation: *flowers of sulfur.* —*v.i.* **13.** to produce flowers, as a plant; blossom; come to full bloom. **14.** to come out into full development; mature: *Ideas flower under favorable conditions.* —*v.t.* **15.** to cover or deck with flowers. **16.** to decorate with a floral design. [ME *flour* flower, best of anything < OF *flor, flour, flur* < L *flōr-* (s. of *flōs*). Cf. BLOSSOM]

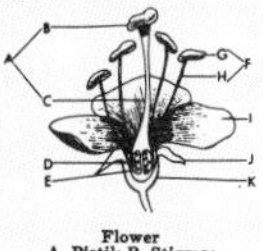

Flower
A, Pistil; B, Stigma; C, Style; D, Ovule; E, Ovary; F, Stamen; G, Anther; H, Filament; I, Petal; J, Sepal; K, Receptacle

gen·ius (jēn′yəs), *n.*, *pl.* **gen·ius·es** for 2, 3, 8, **gen·i·i** (jē′nē ī′) for 6, 7, 9. **1.** an exceptional natural capacity of intellect, especially as shown in creative and original work in art, music, etc. **2.** a person having such capacity. **3.** a person having extraordinarily high intelligence, esp. one with an I.Q. of 140 or above. **4.** natural ability or capacity; strong inclination: *a special genius for pediatric medicine.* **5.** distinctive character or spirit, as of a nation, period, language, etc. **6.** the guardian spirit of a place, institution, etc. **7.** either of two mutually opposed spirits, one good and the other evil, supposed to attend a person throughout his life. **8.** a person who strongly influences for good or ill the character, conduct, or destiny of a person, place, or thing: *Rasputin, the evil genius of Russian politics.* **9.** Usually **genii.** any demon or spirit, esp. a jinn. [< L: tutelary deity or genius of a person; cf. GENUS]
—**Syn. 4.** gift, talent, aptitude, faculty.

grad·u·ate (*n., adj.* graj′o͞o it, -āt′; *v.* graj′o͞o āt′), *n., adj., v.,* **-at·ed, -at·ing.** —*n.* **1.** a person who has received a degree or diploma on completing a course of study, as in a university, college, or school. **2.** a student who holds the first or bachelor's degree and is studying for an advanced degree. **3.** a cylindrical or tapering graduated container, used for measuring. —*adj.* **4.** of, pertaining to, or involved in academic study beyond the first or bachelor's degree: *the graduate school of business; a graduate student.* **5.** graduated (def. 3). —*v.i.* **6.** to receive a degree or diploma on completing a course of study (often fol. by *from*): *She graduated from Sweet Briar in 1962.* **7.** to pass by degrees; change gradually. —*v.t.* **8.** to confer a degree upon, or to grant a diploma to, at the close of a course of study, as in a university, college, or school: *Cornell graduated eighty students with honors.* **9.** to graduate from: *She graduated college in 1950.* **10.** to arrange in grades or gradations; establish gradation in. **11.** to divide into or mark with degrees or other divisions, as the scale of a thermometer. [< ML *graduāt(us)* (ptp. of *graduāre*), equiv. to *grād(us)* GRADE, step + *-u-* thematic vowel + *-ātus* -ATE[1]] —**grad′u·a′tor,** *n.*

he·don·ism (hēd′ᵊniz′əm), *n.* **1.** the doctrine that pleasure or happiness is the highest good. **2.** devotion to pleasure as a way of life: *The later Roman emperors were notorious for their hedonism.* [< Gk *hēdon(ē)* pleasure + -ISM] —**he′don·ist,** *n., adj.* —**he′do·nis′tic,** *adj.* —**he′do·nis′ti·cal·ly,** *adv.*

lov·er (luv′ər), *n.* **1.** a person who is in love, esp. a man in love with a woman. **2.** a man amorously involved with a woman not his wife; paramour. **3. lovers,** a man and woman in love with each other or having a love affair. **4.** a person who has a strong predilection or liking for something, as specified: *a lover of music.* **5.** a person who loves, esp. a person who has or shows affectionate regard for others: *a lover of mankind.* [ME; see LOVE, -ER[1]] —**lov′er·less,** *adj.* —**lov′er·like′,** *adj.*

mug·wump (mug′wump′), *n.* *U.S* **1.** a Republican who refused to support the party nominee, James G. Blaine, in the presidential campaign of 1884. **2.** a person who acts as an independent or affects superiority, esp. in politics. **3.** a person who is unable to make up his mind on an issue, esp. in politics; one who is neutral on a controversial issue. [< Algonquian (Massachusetts): lit., great man] —**mug′wump′er·y, mug′wump′ism,** *n.* —**mug′wump′i·an,** *adj.* —**mug′wump′ish,** *adj.*

mu·tu·al·ism (myo͞o′cho͞o ə liz′əm), *n.* **1.** a relationship between two species of organisms in which both benefit from the association. **2.** the doctrine that the interdependence of social elements is the primary determinant of individual and social relations, esp. the theory that common ownership of property, or collective effort and control governed by sentiments of brotherhood and mutual aid will be beneficial to both the individual and society. **3.** *Sociol.* the force or principle of mutual aid. [MUTUAL + -ISM] —**mu′tu·al·ist,** *n.* —**mu′tu·al·is′tic,** *adj.*

O·lym·pi·an (ō lim′pē ən), *adj.* **1.** pertaining to Mount Olympus or dwelling thereon, as the gods of classical Greece. **2.** pertaining to Olympia in Elis. **3.** of, resembling, characteristic of, or suitable to the gods of Olympus; majestic; aloof; incomparably superior: *a landscape of Olympian beauty; an Olympian disregard for everyday matters.* —*n.* **4.** an Olympian deity. **5.** a contender in the Olympic Games. **6.** a native or inhabitant of Olympia. [< LL *Olympiān(us)*, equiv. to L *Olympi(us)* (< Gk *Olýmpios*, deriv. of *Ólymp(os)* OLYMPUS) + *-iānus* -IAN] —**O·lym′pi·an·ly,** *adv.*

Om (ōm), *n.* *Hinduism.* a mantric word thought to be a complete expression of Brahman and interpreted as having three sounds representing Brahma or creation, Vishnu or preservation, and Siva or destruction, or as consisting of the same three sounds, representing waking, dreams, and deep sleep, along with the following silence, which is fulfillment. Also, **Aum.** [< Skt]

om·pha·lo·skep·sis (om′fə lō skep′sis), *n.* contemplation of one's navel as part of a mystical exercise. [OMPHALO- + Gk *sképsis* act of looking]

peace (pēs), *n., v.,* **peaced, peac·ing,** *interj.* —*n.* **1.** the normal, nonwarring condition of a nation, group of nations, or the world. **2.** an agreement or treaty between warring or antagonistic nations, groups, etc., to end hostilities and abstain from further fighting or antagonism: *the Peace of Ryswick.* **3.** a state of mutual harmony between people or groups, esp. in personal relations: *Try to live in peace with your neighbors.* **4.** the normal freedom from civil commotion and violence of a community; public order and security: *He was arrested for being drunk and breaking the peace.* **5.** cessation of or freedom from any strife or dissension. **6.** freedom of the mind from annoyance, distraction, anxiety, an obsession, etc.; tranquility; serenity. **7.** a state of tranquility or serenity: *May he rest in peace.* **8.** a state or condition conducive to, proceeding from, or characterized by tranquility: *the peace of a mountain resort.* **9.** silence; stillness: *The cawing of a crow broke the afternoon's peace.* **10.** (*cap., italics*) a comedy (421 B.C.) by Aristophanes. **11. hold one's peace,** to refrain from or cease speaking; keep silent: *He told her to hold her peace until he had finished.* **12. keep the peace,** to maintain order; cause to refrain from creating a disturbance: *Several officers of the law were on hand to keep the peace.* **13. make one's peace,** to become reconciled; acquiesce: *He repaired the fence he had broken and made his peace with the neighbor on whose property it stood.* **14. make peace,** to ask for or arrange a cessation of hostilities or antagonism. —*v.i.* **15.** *Obs.* to be or become silent. —*interj.* **16.** keep still! silence! [ME *pes* < OF, var. of *pais* < L *pāc(em)*, acc. of *pax* peace; akin to PACT] —**peace′less,** *adj.* —**peace′less·ness,** *n.* —**peace′like′,** *adj.*
—**Syn. 2.** armistice, truce, pact, accord. **3.** rapport. **6.** calm, quiet. —**Ant. 6.** insecurity, disturbance.

Thoth (thōth, tōt), *n.* *Egyptian Religion.* the god of wisdom, learning, and magic, the inventor of numbers and letters, and scribe of all the gods, represented as a man with the head either of an ibis or of a baboon: identified by the Greeks with Hermes.

wom·an·pow·er (wo͝om′ən pou′ər), *n.* potential or actual power from the endeavors of women: *the utilization of womanpower during a great national emergency.* [WOMAN + POWER]

x, **1.** an unknown quantity or a variable. **2.** ex[1] (def. 1). **3.** experimental. **4.** a sign used at the end of letters, telegrams, etc., to indicate a kiss. **5.** a sign indicating multiplication; times: $8 \times 8 = 64$. **6.** a sign used between figures indicating dimensions: 3″ × 4″ (read: "three by four inches"); 3″ × 4″ × 5″ (read: "three by four by five inches"). **7.** power of magnification: *50x telescope.* **8.** (used as a signature by an illiterate person.) **9.** crossed with. **10.** out of; foaled by: *a colt by Flag-a-way x Merrylegs.* **11.** (used to indicate choice, as on a ballot, examination, etc.) **12.** (used to indicate an error or incorrect answer, as on a test.) **13.** *Math.* (in Cartesian coordinates) the *x*-axis. **14.** *Chess.* captures. **15.** a person, thing, agency, factor, etc., of unknown identity.

Yin and Yang (yin′ and yäng′, yang′), (in Chinese philosophy and religion) two principles, one negative, dark, and feminine (**Yin**), and one positive, bright, and masculine (**Yang**), whose interaction influences the destinies of creatures and things.

The $4 words shown here are available wherever meaningful sweat shirts are sold. But if they don't grab you, try this: pick any definition you like from the 260,000-plus entries in *The Random House Dictionary of the English Language* (the first new major dictionary in a generation). Write the word you choose below and send it to us along with $19.95. In two weeks you'll very likely have the only sweat shirt of its kind in the world. Make your check payable to:

Eagle Shirtmakers, Dept. R
Quakertown, Pa.

My word ____________________

Name ____________________

Address ____________________

City ________ State ________ Zip # ________

Small ☐ Med. ☐ Large ☐ Extra Large ☐

DUSTIN HOFFMAN, STARRING IN "THE GRADUATE," A JOSEPH E. LEVINE PRESENTATION FOR EMBASSY PICTURES RELEASE.

25.

Plus C'est
la Même Chose

Costume is custom. It is a corporate mask.
A put-on, not a take-off.

WOMEN, BEWARE WOMEN

"You Think She's Yours, But She Could Turn on You in a Second." (<u>Family Circle</u>, August, 1968)

The old gray mare came roaring out of the wilderness.

So friend of vegetables, you long cold cat you. (Joyce)

Clothing is anti-environment, is vestment, investment.

Calypso is Greek for "covering"; i.e., Circe the witch, capable of endless metamorphoses. Breaker of cities.

The Circe episode of <u>Ulysses</u> is nighttown: The world of dreams, <u>coutume</u> repeats and transformations of daily events, extensions of our own skins. Joyce presents the psychic purge, private and corporate, in a fantastic series of <u>coutumes</u>.

Start the New Year with a New Face. Was this the face that launched a thousand skirtmishes?

Revlon proposes: Lashes to sweep him off his feet.

Imitation is the sincerest form of battery.

for women who
hunt for the
best in a
$1 stocking

beauty mist.

beautifully fashioned, perfectly fitting stockings

NOAH'S ARCHETYPES

"Here she comes full sail." (Congreve's Mourning Bride)

Avril here features the iconic Aubrey Beardsley design of the 1890's. Beardsley, appropriately, was a sort of "she."

"A boat is called a She because there's always a great deal of bustle about her—because there's usually a gang of men around her... because she shows her topsides, hides her bottom, and when coming into port always heads for the buoys." (Bangor Daily News)

Might as well start with the human body as vesture for man's wayward spirit! (The Golden Ass of Apuleius)

Carlyle's Sartor Resartus followed in the tracks of the eighteenth-century Swedenborg zeitgeist theory of Age Garb (or garbage); i.e., all human institutions from language to tweezers are extensions of, and weapons of, the human body.

New technologies = new environments, new social dress. (Greek word perivallo to hit from all sides.) New environments stun men. They are the Emperor's new clothes.

Fashion is making via facio=fiction=fake.

Joyce's Martello Tower was built to fend off Napoleon. His Marion Tweedy (Mrs. Bloom) spins an endless Penelope's web of emotional labyrinths.

When the tag goes on, it will read

AVRIL

Hi-Performance rayon

Avril rayon makes the fashion statement of the times. It takes long or the short of it. Styled throwbacks to yesteryear or signs of things to come. And gives it the feeling of now. Carefree and comfy. Light and lively. Free. And eager to stand alone or blend, to make out of great wovens or knits. So go the way. Break out in Avril hi-performance rayon. And let yourself fly.

MINI

Designer Adapts Nuns' Garb for Public. Hey nonny nunny.

Wear the Yellow Pages Out for $1.

Poster Dresses Are Here.

Miniskirts are not a fashion. They are a return to tribal corporate costume. In tribal societies men and women wear the same short skirts. There is no change.

Playboy and hot photography pushed the West over the sex hump into non-sex.

The miniskirt is not sexy. Sex does not interest tribal man as a theme. Was John Donne the first to use "sex" in our fragmented sense?

"True Wit is Nature to advantage dress'd, What oft was thought, but ne'er so well express'd." (Pope)

The power of names to create new public dimensions of fashion got a QED endorsement from Twiggy and Penny Tree, innovators of the miniskirt.

With Different Aims, Two Sisters Are Hitting Their Targets. (N.Y. Times, Feb. 21/68)

Don't feed a turtle... wear one

Turtle soup-er. Recipe for groovy summers, and just part of the cover-up epidemic that's sweeping the beaches. It's contagious... expose yourself at Macy's-by-the-Sea, where you'll find not only the turtles, but exciting new tunics, romantic swim-dresses, bitsy bikinis, and nifty-shifts. Everything's new. The fabrics. The colors. The ship-shapes by Cole of California, Rose Marie Reid, Jantzen, Catalina, Brigance, Peter Pan, Roxanne, Sandcastle, Sirena, Darlene. Everything you'll need to turn a shore thing into a sure thing. Macy's-by-the-Sea, Third Floor, Herald Square, and the Macy's near you.

It's Take-a-Turtle-To-The-Beach Week at Macy's-by-the-Sea

EXTENSION OF SKIN

The Fur-lined Teacup and the Cloud-lined Bra.

Unions Hassle Over Falsie Rights.

Women in 1880 wore 14 pounds of clothes— the weight of the cover of a prairie schooner.

Boredom Turned Clothes Hobby into Big Business—Mrs. Florence Eiseman, the Norman Norell of Children's Clothes. (N.Y. Times, June 24/68)

Banks, as the tailors of endless new environmental clothing by investment in new technologies, could never have had a more magically appropriate name than the Bank of England: "The Old Lady of Threadneedle Street."

Like the Prankquean, The Old Lady is a major character in Finnegans Wake.

The Op Art clothing seen here is a direct extension of the TV screen to other materials.

"Nothing so true as what you once let fall,
'Most Women have no Characters at all.'
Matter too soft a lasting mark to bear,
And best distinguish'd by black, brown or fair.
How many pictures of one Nymph we view,
All how unlike each other, all how true!" (Pope)

rose marie reid takes Op Art out of the gallery and gives it to every girl on the beach! What's wilder yet is to mix these cotton prints in swimsuits, cover-ups and accessories. From Deep Summer Collection. "O-Oh-Seven" button-down shirt $14. "Myopia" bikiniest bikini $15, head-kerchief $5. For the name of a store nearest you, write to Rose Marie Reid, Dept. G, 5200 W. Century Boulevard, Los Angeles, California 90045.

UPTIGHT

'66 Was the Year of the Beatles, '67 Drugs— and '68? (<u>N.Y. Times</u>, Dec. 31/67)

Poodles and Psychiatrists Are Taking Over New York. (<u>Saturday Evening Post</u> ad, which goes on: "These are the depressing words of Mr. Horace Sutton — a neurotic New Yorker who hates New York. Hates it. Hates it. <u>Hates</u> it.)

The <u>Saturday Evening Post</u> performed on itself the same kind of psychic purge that England has done via London Bridge and the <u>Queen Mary</u>. It sloughed off two million subscribers in order to show a better face to the world.

Tale of a New Tub. Psychiatry is merging with the Esalen-type communal bathtubs, watered by tears and stirred by tribal sobs. The private couch yields to the corporate tub.

Soon New York will be dismantled girder by girder. Kuwait billionaires will use the Empire State Building as a kiddie playpen.

The underwater landscape has already been littered by skindivers.

When Arab women first took off their veils, they felt 30 feet tall. They couldn't cross a street. Clothes make the gal.

Scuba·duba·(do)

Do the scuba bit. Splash, dash, a magenta sash . . . All this makes a vacation in Acapulco. Fly with us to our country and your favorite resort. Leave in the AM—we'll greet you with "Buenos Dias." Leave in the PM—we'll greet you with "Buenos Noches." You'll hear and feel Mexico sooner, Amigo, when you visit Mexico in Mexico's own airline . . . See your friendly travel agent or call 274-9700 — **AERO-NAVES DE MEXICO,** 500 Fifth Avenue — scu-be-do-be-do!

26.

Help Beautify
Junk Yards

The TV child, rich or poor, shares the same
new information world. The old hardware
can't match the riches of TV software imagery,
whether at school or at the A & P.

THROW SOMETHING LOVELY AWAY TODAY

"We have no art. We do everything as well as possible." (Balinese saying)

Oral societies regard the environment as art. Artists and archeologists see a world of order and significant social gesture in any midden heap.

The Russian splitting of the Communist world was via hardware. Russia never had a nineteenth century of hardware consumer services. Czechoslovakia did. The electric juxtaposition of Russia and Czechoslovakia destroys the Russian image.

The United States splits the Western world over Vietnam because the tribal communism of the Orient now looks better to American kids than the software communism of American suburbia. The electric juxtaposition of East and West destroys the Western image.

When images of identity are endangered, violence begins.

The city's first summer musical concert...was canceled yesterday when striking garbage collectors marched in front of a portable bandstand. (Toronto Globe and Mail, June 27 / 68)

Let's program the whole environment like a double helix.

FEBRUARY 1967
PRICE 75c
GREAT BRITAIN 4/6

THE MAGAZINE FOR MEN

**The New American Woman:
through at 21.**

see page 57

MEETING OF HARDWARE AND SOFTWARE

When the old political machines meet the new electric environment strange hybrid images emerge. Barbwire conventions, etc.

Acceleration of transactions not only eliminates the stock exchanges and the gold standard, but also age categories.

A Mobil Gas ad portrays an erotic clutch in a fast-moving car: "Till Death Do Us Part."

A TV Guide ad for the Olympics indicates the normal meeting of hard and software: Help Bring Gold Back into the U.S. (medals).

"Go across the full length of the U.S. and what do you find....The bulldozer and the pneumatic drill, energy, noise, change, the fantastic beauty of the Los Angeles Center and the slums of Watts." (James Reston, Toronto Globe and Mail, March 8/68)

314

Till death us do part.

It may be beautiful to die for love in a poem.

But it's ugly and stupid to die for love in a car.

Yet how many times have you seen (or been) a couple more interested in passion than in passing? Too involved with living to worry about dying?

As a nation, we are allowing our young to be buried in tons of steel. And not only the reckless lovers—the just plain nice kids as well.

Everyone is alarmed about it. No one really knows what to do. And automobile accidents, believe it or not, continue to be the leading cause of death among young people between 15 and 24 years of age.

Parents are alarmed and hand over the keys to the car anyway.

Insurance companies are alarmed and charge enormous rates which deter no one.

Even statisticians (who don't alarm easily) are alarmed enough to tell us that by 1970, 14,450 young adults will die in cars each year.

(Just to put those 14,450 young lives in perspective, that is about 4 times the number of young lives we have lost so far in Viet Nam.)

Is it for this that we spent our dimes and dollars to all but wipe out polio? Is it for this that medical science conquered diphtheria and smallpox?

What kind of society is it that keeps its youngsters alive only long enough to sacrifice them on the highway?

Yet that is exactly what's happening. And it's incredible.

Young people should be the best drivers, not the worst.

They have the sharper eyes, the steadier nerves, the quicker reflexes. They probably even have the better understanding of how a car works.

So why?

Are they too dense to learn? Too smart to obey the obvious rules? Too sure of themselves? Too un-sure? Or simply too young and immature?

How can we get them to be old enough to be wise enough before it's too late?

One way is by insisting on better driver training programs in school. Or *after* school. Or after work. Or during summers.

By having stricter licensing requirements. By rewarding the good drivers instead of merely punishing the bad ones. By having uniform national driving laws (which don't exist today). By having radio and TV and the press deal more with the problem. By getting *you* to be less complacent.

Above all, by setting a decent example ourselves.

Nobody can stop young people from driving. And nobody should. Quite the contrary. The more exposed they become to sound driving techniques, the better they're going to be. (Doctors and lawyers "practice;" why not drivers?)

We at Mobil are not preachers or teachers. We sell gasoline and oil for a living and we want everyone to be a potential customer.

If not today, tomorrow. And we want everyone, young and old, to have his fair share of tomorrows. **Mobil**

We want you to live.

LITTLE GIRL'S LEG IS IN

Meantime, big girl's friend is sticking out: "A girl's best friend is not necessarily diamonds, not when their value is declining."

A sportswear sweater is offered as "ready to captain a windjammer, or sail the seven seas solo, or cruise through geometry without any angling at all."

Message to deep-sea diver: "Surface at once. Ship is sinking."

SHOES & HANDBAGS

THE NEST EGG

New pound notes, instead of "will pay to bearer," now say, "Watch this space."

"Money is the American god, and therefore provides the only hope of unity between white and black." (Negro saying)

Gibraltar Feels the Squeeze: A more implacable opponent than Spain in 1968—the spiraling cost of living on the Rock. (The Nassau Guardian and Bahamas Observer, Jan. 29/68)

Ireland is one of the few countries in the world where People Talk Louder than Money. (N.Y. Times, tourist ad)

"Money is an incompletely unified system, a search for its single purpose, a blind alley." (Karl Polanyi)

The poor man's credit card.

Nest eggs were lures for hens to lay. How did they ever get into the role of storehouse?

The Rich Man's Vacation Now at Popular Prices. (ad)

Still getting ready to live?

Does your wallet look like you need a raise?

You look like you've lived up to all those prophecies in the high school yearbook.

Until you pull out your wallet. Even when it's stuffed with cash and credit cards, those torn seams look pretty unsuccessful.

Why don't you give them up for the Convertible billfold by Lord Buxton?

The Convertible has a good, comfortable feeling in your hand. It smells like new shoes. And it has a special removable section

for credit cards and photographs.

Before you go out and get the Convertible, if you really want a raise, maybe you should show the wallet you have now to your boss.

The Convertible, from $5.00. Matching Key-Tainer, from $3.00.

The Convertible° by **LORD BUXTON**°
BEST FOR YOUR MONEY

WHAT'S YOUR LION (bag)?

Now Albert 'ad 'eard about lions
'ow they was 'orrible and fierce...

When lions have been caged or enclosed, their sensory lives change as much as that of humans. They cease to be suspicious and alert with all their senses. They regard their keepers as extensions of themselves. The keepers, as new environments, have "swallowed" the lions.

When a man's interests swallow him he is
said to have "a bag." "What's your bag?"
is the new way of saying a total environment.

"What's your line?" used to indicate a specialty.

The Dreyfus Fund is a mutual investment fund in which the management hopes to make your money grow, and takes what it considers sensible risks in that direction. Your securities dealer or his mutual fund representative will be happy to give you a prospectus.

DREYFUS FUND INC

MAKING IT

From Beat to Beatitude—Just a stand-by in the waiting room of Life.

McLuhan to customs officer: "Yes, I'm acquainted with Dr. Tim
O'Leary."

Officer: "Okay. Then were's the LL.D. you were
heard to say you were picking up in
Vancouver?"

**The transition from hardware service
environments to software service
environments was dramatized serendipity-
style by the coincidence of f.s.d. (the old
hardware) with all the aggression of
nineteenth-century enterprise, and LSD (the
new software) with all the passivity of the
inner trip. The gap between these modes
carries a high charge of communication, i.e.,
of ferment and transformation.**

Invisible to accountants, actuaries and bureaucrats is the point of
reversal in service environments. With industrial or hardware
enviromnents, there is a point when services available to ordinary
workers far exceed the means of the greatest private wealth to
provide such services for itself. That is the invisible moment of change
from individualism to communism. It had occurred in England by
1830 at the latest — well before Marx. Under electric or software
conditions the point of change is confused and concealed by the
hybridizing of hard and software.

**Today no billionaire can afford a private
electric service of any kind—not a world
telegraph nor world telephone nor any later
development. These services, however, are
practically free to the ordinary person.**

I BOUGHT MY OFFICE FURNITURE

I LEASED MY OFFICE FURNITURE

You could be losing money right now just by *owning* your office furniture. It's happening to some of the smartest people. People who've simply never thought of an alternative.

The cost of leasing furniture can be far less than the cost of owning it—for a whole string of complicated reasons that have to do with taxes, credit, insurance, maintenance, inflation, interest, amortization and where your working capital comes from.

It would take a small book to tell the whole story.

You can get that small book *free* by asking us for a copy. Write or phone: **The Itkins:** 250 Madison Avenue (212) 686-3975
Open every Saturday until 3 P.M.

27

Software

"Go across the full length of the U. S. and what do you find...The bulldozer and the pneumatic drill, energy, noise, change, the fantastic beauty of the Los Angeles Center and the slums of Watts." (James Reston, <u>Toronto Globe and Mail</u>, March 8/68)

"THE HELIOTROPICAL NOUGHTTIME"

"The hands are the hands of Esau but the voice is the voice of Jacob."

"The nervous system is the greatest of all poems." (Paul Valéry)

I.e., The new electric environment is a corporate poem.

"The instrument of crisis in the White House is the telephone." (Life, July 5/68)

Rock as Salvation: "The idea of the new pop music as a religious force...The Rock Experience..."pounded by volume, riddled by light, an imitation of engulfment." (Benjamin de Mott, N.Y. Times magazine, Aug. 25/68)

"Come in under the shadow of this red rock." (The Waste Land)

"Professor Morse's telegraph is not only an era in the transmission of intelligence, but it has originated in the mind an entirely new class of ideas, a new species of consciousness." (New York magazine, Aug. 18/68)

"Morrison's eyes glow as he discusses the Apollonian Dionysian struggle for life's force. It's easy to guess which side he's on." (The Shaman As Superstar by Richard Goldstein, New York magazine, Aug. 5/68)

The Sun Set for Night People

The Sun Set isn't just for sunny days. It's a dream on moony nights. The black screen makes blacks blacker and whites whiter in any light. And, since it runs on rechargeable batteries as well as AC current, you don't have to sit home at night watching television. You can go out and watch the Sun Set. **SONY**

PICKING PETALS OFF A DAISY
OR MISSION IMPOSSIBLE?

Trumpets of Chance Heralding New Era in Wall Street Arena. The business community was shocked last week when three leaders of the Securities Industry raised the Specter of a Wall Street without a New York Stock Exchange. (<u>N.Y. Times</u>, Aug. 25/68)

London Bridge Is Not Falling Down: It has been sold as a curio for 2,460,000 dollars to an oil co. (<u>Life</u>)

Inability to distinguish the old hardware service environment has involved the U.S. in a frantic struggle with the tribal communism of South East Asia. The same impercipience has blocked awareness of the new tribal communism surging in the sensibilities of the TV teen-agers of affluent suburbia.

In electric systems communication is by gaps, switches and transistors.

Today he's 1 bath, 2 naps, 3 meals and 137 Great Discoveries older

(today you're 24 hours closer to your next birthday)

My! How he has grown. So has the need to provide your family with the protection they surely ought to have.

Don't let yet another year pass. Don't let another birthday pass. Don't let another *day* pass. See your Prudential agent soon. Plain fact is,

you'll never pay less for insurance than *right now*. From your Prudential "pro"— have a happy birthday.

THE PRUDENTIAL INSURANCE COMPANY OF AMERICA

GOING, GOING, GONG

**The new electronic harems or "conglomerates,"
as they are known in the business world,
produce strange bedfellows: Colt is Seeking
Electric Concern. (<u>N.Y. Times</u> Aug. 21/68)**

Feats of rear-view mirrorism to match those of David Sarnoff are
described in <u>Horizon</u> (Summer, 1968) under the heading, Man at
War with Nature.

**Since Sputnik there is no Nature. Nature is an
item contained in a man-made environment
of satellites and information. Goals have
now to be replaced by the sensory reprogram-
ming of total environments and DNA particles,
alike. The earth is an old nose cone.**

The old hardware centralized families and businesses. The new
software diffuses both into an information environment:
Where the Gauguin maids
In the banyan shades
Wear palm-leaf drapery.
— T. S. Eliot, <u>Fragment of an Agon</u>

"*The Ten Commandments* was a success because we studied what people like. Gulf+Western's doing the same now with *True Grit* and *Paint Your Wagon.*"

"At Paramount in the old days—and I started in 1912—we knew our own judgment wasn't enough. We studied the reactions of the public. On opening nights, I didn't watch the picture. I watched the audience.

"*The Ten Commandments* was a success because first we studied what people like. The stories. The cast.

"Gulf+Western's doing the same now with pictures like *True Grit, Paint Your Wagon* and *Romeo and Juliet.* They're even doing it more intensively than in the past.

"They're also getting the best people. They pick and pick until they find the best man for a job. They look for know-how, experience, and enthusiasm. And show business, you know, lives on enthusiasm.

"When we agreed to merge Paramount with them, Gulf+Western's Mr. Bluhdorn and I shook hands and he said to me, 'All we can promise is you'll be as proud of Paramount as you ever were.'

"And I am."

Adolph Zukor, Founder
Paramount Pictures Corporation

Gulf+Western
The 21st Century Company

THE MOB
BLAMES TV FOR VIOLENCE

TV will produce a reversion to civilized book values by sheer reversal of itself. TV automatically makes the tribal man superior. The iconic, tribal mask of the oriental and the Negro belongs to the TV medium. The chiaroscuro of the white face fails even on black-and-white TV.

As with radio, TV as software gets to backward areas before the old hardware of consumer goods and services: e.g., TV: Hunger Amid Plenty. (N.Y. Times, May 22/68)

The TV child, rich or poor, shares the same new information world. The old hardware can't match the riches of TV software imagery, whether at school or at the A & P. The result is confusion and anger in tribal and suburban worlds alike.

Life, August 30, 1968, spent much space on the tribal world of the Mafia. These men of an ancient oral cultural are as unable to adjust to visual, book values as our children of the TV generation. They are killers with a code. When the code is violated by amateurs they are confused: "If you want to get rid of him, hit him clean....What's all this here rigamajig? I don't know if they saw television or what."

The mob now thinks like our sociologists.

Sometimes a television set
can light up a whole city

When a message is powerful enough...if it is told well enough
...it can enlighten a home, a neighborhood, a whole community.

It happened in Baltimore...with WJZ-TV's coverage of
the civil rights struggle.

It happened in Pittsburgh...when KDKA-TV and KDKA
examined growing unemployment.

It happened in San Francisco...with the KPIX series on
mentally retarded children.

It happened in Boston...when WBZ-TV and WBZ took a
searching look at morality in government.

It happened in Fort Wayne, New York, Chicago...with
WOWO, WINS, WIND.

It's happening in Cleveland now. A KYW-TV and KYW

series has already begun to reveal the blight of poverty in a
major city.

These are all Group W stations. In the past year and a
half they have received broadcasting's top awards. Including
the duPont, the Peabody, the Sigma Delta Chi, the Sloan, the
Edison, and the Ohio State.

Group W stations are uniquely equipped to play a vital
role in their communities. As members of the Group, they
have creative, managerial, and financial resources greater
than any individual station, plus a local impact no network
can match. Important, meaningful programming in the public interest is one more reason why the Group is a vital third
force in broadcasting today.

WESTINGHOUSE BROADCASTING COMPANY

WBZ·WBZ-TV BOSTON ·WINS NEW YORK·WJZ-TV BALTIMORE·KDKA·KDKA-TV PITTSBURGH·KYW·KYW-TV CLEVELAND·WOWO FORT WAYNE·WIND CHICAGO·KPIX SAN FRANCISCO

THE ELECTRIC INFAMY ENVIRONMENT

"We are the primitives of a new kind of culture." (Boccioni)

The Whole of The Human Age by P. Wyndham Lewis is a science fiction entertainment about the transition of Pullman and Satters (bureaucratic refugees from the old hardware environment) to the Magnetic City (software) dominated by the Satanic intelligence of Sammael. Straddling these worlds is the wonderful Buffoon, the Bailiff. He is the type of the old press lord, a Beaverbrook colonial who uses the telegraph cum ink and paper to create huge storms and panic in the old hardware environment. The Bailiff is the natural inheritor of a defaulting and somnambulist world. The Bailiff's newspaper hullabaloo is a pale premonition of The Bomb. The Bomb is electric software. It inspires nightmares of population explosions in the old nineteenth-century minds. There is no finish line.